Yoga For I

Your Guide To Mast
Strengthening Your Body, Calming Your
Mind And Be Stress-Free!

Emily Oddo

Dedication

To my sons: Justin and Anne, you bring me more joy than I can ever describe.

To Anthony: my best friend, business partner, and Husband, you are more than I can ever ask for in a spouse. I thank God every day for the opportunity to look into those beautiful green eyes, you are a piece of me. To my loving parents: who have been together for 25+ years, you are the perfect example of love and companionship.

To my friends Kellie, Jason and Jenny: I love you guys!.

Introduction

Dear Listener,

I want to thank you and congratulate you for buying this book, *"Yoga For Beginners: Your Guide To Master Yoga Poses While Strengthening Your Body, Calming Your Mind And Be Stress- Free!"*

I think you will agree with me when I say, the world is a pretty crazy place. I mean we all wake up early in the morning, take our breakfast, disappear into our daily responsibilities (which can be work or school), return home, try to get some few hours of sleep and then wake up and repeat everything again.

What are we really doing to ourselves? We have made ourselves so busy that we have lost touch with our inner selves; which is okay except for the fact that, that type of life is affecting our health negatively by piling up stress in your body and mind.

You know what we need, a breather and this guide has the perfect one for you. YOGA!

Yes, you heard me. For a long time now, yoga has been known to work wonders on the body and mind. Basically, it helps you get in touch with your inner self in a process that releases stress from your body, calms your mind and boosts your strength. After a session of yoga, you glow and feel light. Now, who wouldn't want that?

This guide will introduce you to this magical method known as yoga. By reading it, you will get to know the history of yoga, the benefits of yoga, what to expect from yoga classes and what you need to start practicing it. You will also learn some yoga postures and routines that you can do to free your mind from stress while strengthening your body.

Are you ready to learn how to channel your inner yogi?

Thanks again for downloading this book. I hope you enjoy it!

Emily Oddo

Buy the Audio version of this book by clicking here:
https://itunes.apple.com/us/audiobook/
yoga-for-beginners-your-guide-to-master-yoga-poses/
id1441152740

Section 1: A Deep Understanding Of Yoga

Before continue, please refer to your audiobook companion PDF that comes free with your purchase of this audiobook to see and learn all the Yoga poses, explained with images.

By definition, yoga is a Hindu system that aims at achieving the spiritual union of your inner self with the Supreme Being in a form of complete tranquility and awareness. It does this through intense concentration, meditation and exercise practices that involve controlled breathing and postures. In simple terms, Yoga is all about connecting your body and mind through breathing and movements that relax the mind and increase the level of flexibility and fitness in your body.

To some, yoga is just a type of exercise that is used as a pathway to empower you to live a fulfilling, strong and healthy life.

Now you have an idea of what yoga is, but where exactly, did it come from and how did it get this popular? Below is a brief history of yoga, which will show you how yoga has developed to the practice that it is today.

History Of Yoga

The practice of yoga began over 5,000 years ago in Northern India; although some researchers say the practice goes as far back as 10,000 years ago. All in all, the Indus-Sarasvati people first developed Yoga.

"Yoga" was first mentioned by the oldest sacred text Rig Veda which was used to collect texts that had rituals, mantras and songs used by Vedic priests. The word yoga was derived from the Sanskrit word yuj which means 'to yoke', 'to unite', or 'to join'. The translation makes sense because in those days (the pre-classical yoga era) yoga was only viewed as a means to unite the body with the spiritual realm.

After the pre-classical yoga era came the classical yoga era; this new era was led and defined by the father of yoga himself, Patanjali's. Patanjali's yoga was presented by sutras, which were the first organized presentation of yoga. Here Patanjali systematized the practice of yoga into an eight-limbed path that was meant to guide people to exceed beyond the mind and achieve yogic freedom or Samadhi which means enlightenment.

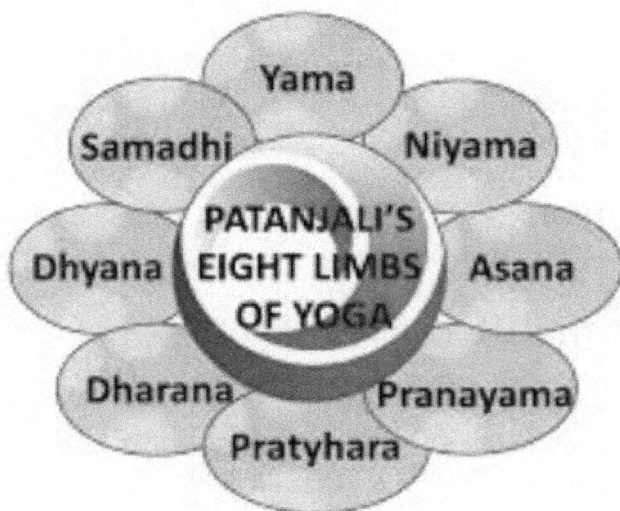

The Eight-Limbed Path

After Patanjali, came the post-classical yoga era where the teachings of the ancient Vedas were rejected. The then yoga masters created their own yoga system that was designed to revitalize the body and prolong life. They developed a physical yoga style with essential techniques of cleansing the body and mind. The method helped practitioners to break out of the knots that fix them to their own physical existence. This style is what later gave birth to what is now known as yoga in the west- Hatha yoga.

Then came the modern period, which started in the 1800s and 1900s; in this era, the yoga masters started spreading the practice of yoga to the west.

- In 1893, Swami Vivekananda gave a yoga lecture on the Parliament of Religions in Chicago.
- In the early 1900s, Swami Sivananda and T. Krishnamacharya promoted hatha yoga in India.
- In 1924, T. Krishnamacharya opened a Hatha yoga school in Mysore-the first yoga school. He produced three students who developed the practice of yoga further.

✓ B.K.S Iyengar created the Iyengar yoga
✓ T.K.V. Desikachar created Viniyoga
✓ K. Pattabhi Jois created the Ashtanga yoga

The yoga styles we have today have evolved from the three students above. The spreading of yoga then continued to trickle down until Indra Devi opened the first yoga studio in Hollywood.

Today the practice of yoga is widespread and there are numerous ways of practicing it; from outdoor venues, schools, community centers, gyms and studios to social media channels like YouTube and online videos.

Now you may have noticed that there is more than one type of yoga as you read the history. The next step of learning about yoga is for you to be enlightened on the types of yoga.

Types Of Yoga

One of the amazing things about yoga is its variety of options when it comes to choosing a method to practice. There are numerous types of yoga, which is amazing because our physical needs are not always the same. Sometimes we want to just stretch, other times we want to do an exercise that will make us sweat while other times we just want to keep fit. Yoga caters for all your needs by providing you with different types of yoga. Here they are:

1. Vinyasa

Vinyasa is a fast-paced type of yoga. Its main aim is usually to link your movement and breath together with a series of yoga poses in a dance-like way. In vinyasa classes, teachers usually put on music that the students use to create a continuous flow from one movement to the other. In short, they match their movements with the beats. In vinyasa, flow is very important and that is why some people refer to vinyasa classes as flow classes.

If you love high-intensity workouts then vinyasa is the thing for you.

2. Hatha

Hatha yoga is a blanket term that stands for different types of yoga. It is among the first yoga styles to be discovered and it is mainly a combination of pranayama (breathing exercise) and asanas (yoga postures). The method is usually about you linking your poses with your breath, which helps bring peace and relaxation to your mind and body.

In a Hatha class, you can expect to hold on to each pose for long and have a slow pace when transitioning from one pose to another. This method is good for you as a beginner because it doesn't put as much pressure on your body as vinyasa does. Therefore, if you are a fun of relaxation yoga then this should be what you want to do.

3. Iyengar

Iyengar yoga is more detailed and precise than Hatha and Vinyasa. In an Iyengar yoga class, you are normally taught to hold on to a pose for a certain period while focusing on the musculoskeletal alignment within each yoga posture.

In this method, you are allowed to use props such as ropes wall, straps, blankets and yoga blocks among others. These props are mostly meant to create a safe and effective environment that helps you be as detail-oriented as you are supposed to be when performing Iyengar yoga movements.

Iyengar yoga is right for you if you love paying attention to details. It is also good if you have injuries.

4. Ashtanga Yoga

Ashtanga yoga is a challenging but orderly type of yoga. This method normally consists of six series of sequenced yoga poses that increase in difficulty as you move from the first pose onwards.

When you attend an Ashtanga class, a yoga teacher normally leads you through the 6 poses while he/she encourages you to breathe over each pose to build internal heat. The idea of this method is to make you perform 6 poses in the exact same order. The process is usually fast, vigorous and challenging.

As a beginner, it is best if you try Hatha or Vinyasa before going to Ashtanga or you can master one series, move to the next and so on until you perfect the method.

5. Bikram Yoga

Bikram yoga normally consists of a series of 26 postures and two breathing techniques that are supposed to be practiced in a room that is 105 degrees and 40 percent humidity for over 1 ½ hours.

It is important to point out that there are numerous types of yoga out there. We cannot highlight all of them so we have just given you the common types of yoga that you need to know as a beginner.

I believe you now know what yoga is, its history and the common types of yoga. The question now is **why should you do yoga? What do you stand to gain?**

Why Yoga?

There was a study that was conducted by Yoga Journal and Yoga Alliance in 2016. The study was called yoga in America. In this study, the researchers found out that there were 36.7 million people practicing yoga in America in that year. This was a whopping 50% increase from 2012. Clearly, something was attracting people to yoga and keeping them there. At the time, it was unclear what it was but it was later discovered that the rise of popularity was mostly attributed to the promising benefits of yoga.

Below is a couple of some of the benefits of yoga, which are going to answer the question 'why should you do yoga'.

1. *It relieves stress*

No one in this world is unfamiliar with stress. We all get frustrated and disappointed with life sometimes. That then makes us stressed. For most people, managing stress is really challenging, which then leads to accumulation of stress for a long time. The accumulation of stress usually causes an imbalance in your nervous system which makes it hard for you to focus, sleep and unwind.

One of the benefits of yoga is its ability to relieve you of stress. The breathing exercises that yoga makes you do usually lower your heart rate, which slowly shifts your nervous system into a relaxed state. It slows down your mental loops of fear, anger, regret and frustration. That then helps you to think clearly, which not only improves your focus but also your sleep. The encouragement of relaxation also helps your body to lower the stress hormone cortisol. That relaxes you further and improves the quality of your life.

1. *It helps to manage diabetes*

If you are at a high risk of diabetes, you will be glad to know that yoga can actually help you reduce your risk of getting diabetes as well as managing it. How? Yoga helps you counter diabetes by reducing the contributing factors that lead to diabetes.

When you practice yoga, you usually do postures that switch back and forth between poses. Some of these poses contract certain areas of your abdomen while others relax those areas. That alternation usually stimulates your pancreas, which increases its oxygen and blood supply. This improves the ability of the organ to produce insulin. The improved production of insulin ensures that your blood sugar levels are well managed and that helps you avoid as well as manage diabetes.

The other contributing factor of diabetes that yoga deals with is stress. More often than not, stress leads to emotional eating of comfort foods high in sugar. The high sugar levels causes your body to produce high levels of insulin to manage your sugar levels. Over time, due to consistent high sugar levels, your pancreas needs to produce more and more insulin, which it is unable to do so leading to pre-diabetes and eventually diabetes if you don't do anything about the situation.

1. *It boosts your immunity*

Practicing yoga constantly makes you move your organs around as you contract and stretch your muscles. When you do that, you usually increase the drainage of lymph in your body. Lymph is a viscous fluid that is rich in immune cells; thus, when it is distributed more through your body, it increases your immune defenses which improves your body's immunity to internal and external attacks.

1. *It makes you happier*

One of the reasons why we as human beings feel sad and angry is because we do not live in the moment. Let me break it down for you; majority of us usually spend time thinking about the future or the past. What this does to us is it keeps us busy planning, worrying or regretting. All of that only increases our nervousness and leaves us feeling miserable.

The practice of yoga usually encourages you to meditate. Meditation helps you to unplug from your thoughts and helps you focus on what is happening in your body and your life. Being in the present is where happiness is found.

1. *Increase Flexibility*

One of the reasons why you should do yoga is so that you can increase your flexibility. Yoga is usually full of postures that work your whole body and this includes even the forgotten joints. This leads to a good sense of balance and harmony. Your muscle groups start working together as opposed to them working against each other; and that is what makes you flexible when you practice yoga.

At the beginning, you might not feel this flexibility but if you keep at it, you will be surprised at how you will gradually loosen up to a point that you are able to do poses that you thought were impossible.

1. *Helps you sleep better*

One of the sort after benefit of yoga is its ability to improve your sleep. Yoga does two things that help you sleep better and deeper. One, it takes you through physically challenging postures a good example being when you are performing Ashtanga and Bikram yoga. This exhausts your body and puts your body in a position where it badly needs sleep in order to reenergize itself.

Secondly, yoga gives you mental relaxation, which provides downtime for your nervous system. This eliminates stress and constant thoughts that keep you awake at night, which means that you get better sleep with it.

1. Builds your muscle strength

You might not know this but muscles don't just make us look good, they also guard us from conditions like back pain and arthritis. One of the best ways to build muscles is through doing yoga. The reason why it's the best is because it helps you with both muscle regeneration and body weight training.

When you practice yoga, you normally bring yourself into positions where your muscles need to support you. Such poses include handstand and downward dog. When you do those types of poses, you usually build your muscle strength using your own body weight.

The good thing about yoga is that it works your whole body targeting all your muscles including the little ones that you might not notice. Yoga also increases the endurance in your muscles by making you hold on to poses for a certain amount of time.

1. Makes you have better sex

Let's be honest, sex is one of the most amazing things that we have in this world. That said, many of us don't get the best out of it. Yoga is good at improving your sex life. How? One, the physical challenging postures like plow pose, chatarunga and the downward dog helps you lift your pelvic floor muscles, which automatically increases your core strength. What this does to you is it helps you go for long when having sex; if you are a man.

Two, yoga helps you have a better orgasm. When you do Mula Bandha, you contract the pubococcygeal muscles in your pelvic region, which creates an energetic seal that locks your breath inside the body. This brings awareness to your pelvic region, which increases your ability to be aroused, and that usually results into a powerful orgasm.

Last but not least, yoga improves your focus, which helps you channel your sex energy on your partner. That helps you to be more in the moment and helps you avoid premature ejaculation.

You now know how beneficial yoga is. Your next question must be how can I start practicing yoga? That question will be fully answered but not before, you get a little bit of introduction to the world of yoga. The next topic is going to orient you into the world of yoga by educating you on things you should know and do before you start practicing yoga.

Buy the Audio version of this book by clicking here:
    https://itunes.apple.com/us/audiobook/
yoga-for-beginners-your-guide-to-master-yoga-poses/
id1441152740

Section 2: Pre-Yoga Orientation And Preparation

Before continue, please refer to your audiobook companion PDF that comes free with your purchase of this audiobook to see and learn all the Yoga poses, explained with images.

As a beginner who is trying on a new activity, it's normal for you to have mixed feelings of nervousness and excitement. That said yoga doesn't need to be nerve-wrecking for you. You can ease into it if you get oriented and prepared for it, which is what this section is going to do.

In this section, you will learn where to start as a beginner, what to expect in yoga and how to approach your first class among many other things. Let's get started then;

Where To Begin As A Newbie In Yoga

The perfect place for you to start when you want to practice yoga is in choosing the type of class that you will do or start with. Basically there are two types of classes; a private session class and a group session class. Below is a brief explanation of each class and their benefits, which will assist you to figure out which one suits you the most.

Group Class Session

A group session is a class of yoga where a number of yoga students gather to be guided on how to do yoga by one yoga teacher. A group class session mostly follows a schedule when it comes to what poses to do on a particular day.

So why choose to do a group class session?

1. *Improves your social life*

A group session of yoga normally provides you with an opportunity to make friends and share your life with a group of like-minded people. This is mostly easy because you share something in common with all the yogis in your class, which is a perfect foundation for friendship and even a relationship.

1. *Offers you a support system*

Most group yoga classes normally have a question answer period at the end of the class. In that period, you and other students get the opportunity to ask and discuss common issues that affect you in yoga. This process is what creates a support system for you because it gives you a platform where you can get help whenever you need. In addition, it helps you learn from other people's problems or challenges.

1. *Helps in consistency*

When you attend a group yoga class, you usually have friends who hold you accountable over everything that you do. These friends are what help you to be consistent in your yoga sessions because if you don't attend, they will be on your case. Your consistency also increases because you form strong bonds with your friends, which makes you not to want to miss a session with them.

Private Sessions

A private yoga session is a class where you get one-on-one instructions from a yoga teacher who is specifically there for you. The yoga teacher is your personal trainer and his/her job is to teach you yoga poses, observe and adjust your poses to make sure you are getting the most out of a yoga session.

So why choose this type of class?

1. *Concentration on your goals*

Everyone who goes to a yoga class usually has a burning reason why they are doing so. Some people do yoga for relaxation purposes, others do it to deal with the back pain they may be experiencing while others do it to get fit and flexible. Basically each student has their specific reasons for doing yoga.

When you choose private sessions as your class, you normally share your goal with your yoga teacher who then prepares a session that is based on your goals. This is impossible in a group yoga class because it has different students with different goals that cannot all be satisfied so they go with a program.

1. *Saves you some embarrassment*

As a beginner in yoga, it is automatic for you to lag behind and do some postures badly when you start yoga. To some of us, this makes us feel embarrassed and even discourages us from attending another yoga session.

Private sessions are beneficial because they give you room to learn without being judged. With them, you can do all the trial and error you want and not only will you not be embarrassed about them but also learn through them at your own pace.

So which is the best between the two methods?

There is no right answer to that question. It all comes down to your personal preference. However, as a beginner it is probably best for you to start with a few private sessions before you can choose the group class sessions.

You can have a private session, where you follow tutorials or you can even use this audiobook to do some poses. The great thing about this option is that it would not cost you anything and you would be able to practice yoga in the comfort of your home.

What To Do Before Your First Yoga Class

The next step after knowing the yoga class to start with, is learning how to approach a yoga class for the first time and knowing what you need to do before then. Below is a list of things that you need to do before your first yoga class:

(i) Set a goal

One of the secret weapons that you should have when going into a yoga class is a goal. A goal is simply what you are aiming to achieve when you practice yoga. As you saw above, everyone who goes into yoga does it for a reason. Yours can be to be fit.

Goals offer you positive stress, which is what you need to succeed in strengthening your body and live a stress free life with yoga. Therefore, before going into a yoga class, you should define your reason for doing yoga and come up with an actionable goal.

(ii) Know what to wear

The basic principle when it comes to what to wear in yoga is, always wear what is comfortable for you. However, some guidelines can help you choose the right clothes to wear when you are starting yoga. Here they are:

- You should wear something that is not too loose. Loose clothes suffocate you during a downward dog pose.
- It is a good idea for you to wear layers on your top half during yoga. This is because it can help you stay warm in savasana and gives you an option of shedding them off when the heat is too much.
- High waist trousers and leggings are highly recommended for yoga. This is because they remove the fear of you exposing

your behind when doing yoga, which heightens your concentration.

Basically a t-shirt and an elastic-waist shorts work perfectly for men. For women a tank top and yoga or leggings pants amazingly works. The last thing to note is yoga is done bare foot so take your socks off when you get into a yoga class.

(iii) Know what to eat before yoga

Every expert in yoga agrees with one thing; you should not eat any heavy food 2 hours before doing yoga. If you do, you and the people around you may pay the price and trust me it won't be pretty.

On a more serious note, doing forward bends and twist on a yoga mat with a full stomach can make you nauseating and uncomfortable and you don't want that.

However, you cannot go to a yoga class on an empty stomach, as you won't last long as yoga needs a lot of energy. Therefore, what you should do is to take a snack like a handful of nuts and yogurt or fruits like bananas and dates, which will provide you with the energy you need without making you full.

(iv) Familiarize yourself with commonly used yoga terms

In order to practice yoga efficiently, you need to learn the commonly used yoga terms; you need to learn the Sanskrit, which is the yoga language. Yoga is normally taught in Sanskrit with a little bit of English. Therefore, if you don't know the yoga language you can be confused the whole time you are in a yoga class. Below are some of the mostly used Sanskrit and there meanings.

- **Asana:** a pose or a posture
- **Tadasana:** mountain pose

- **Savasana:** corpse poses. It's a final resting pose in a yoga class.
- **Prayama:** controlled breathing.
- **Bandha:** tightening of your muscles
- **Namaste:** it's a respectful greeting in yoga
- **Utkatasana:** chair pose
- **Vinyasa:** a series of poses
- **Mantra:** repeating words or syllables
- **Chanting Om:** it is a sound of creation that yogis use to unite energy and bring sacredness into their practices

(v) How to communicate in class

Yoga sessions are very strict when it comes to communication. They don't allow you to talk when a session is in progress. Why, you may wonder? This is because you will distract the class by interfering with other students' concentration. So how are you supposed to communicate in yoga?

The best time for you to communicate with your yoga teacher is before or after a class. For instance, if you are pregnant or you are a beginner, you can approach the teacher before a session and tell them that. They will then find you the necessary props that will make the yoga practice comfortable for you. That is common practice.

Once the yoga session starts, you need to keep quiet and pay attention. However, what if you have something pressing to ask in the middle of a yoga session? What should you do then? If something is important, you can raise your hand and then the teacher will come to you.

(vi) Know what to bring when you go to a yoga room

The only items that you are allowed to bring in a yoga room are usually a bottle of water, a mat and maybe a small towel to wipe your sweat with. As a beginner, you should avoid carrying your phone into a yoga room.. This is because a yoga room is a place where you disconnect yourself from the outside world and a cell phone is a part of your outside world.

What To Expect From Yoga Class As A Beginner

By now, you know that you need to remove your shoes, choose a spot, set your mat and wait for the class to begin when attending a yoga class. However, what should you expect to happen next? Here is a brief explanation of what happens next.

At the beginning of a yoga class, the instructor is going to guide you through some breathing, which he/she will match with your movement. The breathing will bring in some focus, strength and energy, which will calm you down and help you execute each pose well.

The instructor will then make you go through a sequence of poses where you will go from lying down to standing and to sitting. The poses that you will do will all be designed for a specific intention such as to improve your balance, strengthening your body or restoring your energy.

Some instructors demonstrate each and every pose for you. They will walk around and adjust your poses to help you get into proper alignment. If you don't like to be adjusted, you can communicate that to the instructor and he won't assist you. That said when the class is big, instructors don't get the time to demonstrate poses so they just use verbal cues. As a beginner you will be encouraged to use props like blocks and straps on your first day. This is because they are good at assisting you to get the most out of the yoga practice.

Yoga classes end with a few minutes of you lying down with your eyes closed in a pose known as savasana. At this time, you are supposed to let your body and breathing relax. Savasana helps you feel the physical effects of the poses that you have just done.

Once you are through with the savasana, the instructor will bow and say Namaste, which is a gesture word that means "thank you" for coming to practice. The students including you will repeat the word Namaste as a way of thanking the instructor.

How To Improve Your Start

For you to improve how you start in yoga, you must understand some basic do's and don'ts when it comes to yoga. Here are a few do's and don'ts that will ensure your first yoga class goes smoothly.

Do's

- ***Find out if a studio offers yoga mats***

As a beginner, you should call in and find out whether the studio you will go to for your first yoga session provides a yoga mat or not. This is essential because not all studios offer you yoga mats. So you are required to bring yours. Knowing this information in advance is better instead of missing a class because you don't have a yoga mat.

- ***Arrive early in class***

As a beginner, it is important for you to arrive at a yoga class 10-15 minutes early. This is because you are a new student and you need some time to familiarize yourself with the class. Arriving early also gives you time to choose a spot, lay down your mat and maybe do some stretches before the class starts. Basically, it gives you time to settle down. That said, arriving in class early is something that you will need to do from your first class onwards.

- ***Let the instructor know that you are new***

As a newbie, your first yoga class can be more beneficial to you if you inform the instructor that you are a new student. Why? This is because instructors tend to offer you more support when they know you are new. Most often than not, they will concentrate mostly on you and that will come with some extra help that will make your first class better than it could be if you hadn't said a thing.

- *In case you have a condition or an injury let your teacher know*

Doing yoga while you have an injury can be dangerous to your health. For instance, it can cause more pain to your injury and it can worsen your injury. Thus, as a beginner, you should inform the instructor if you have an injury. That way, they will be able to advice you on what to do and what not to do during a yoga class.

Don'ts

- *Never ignore savasana*

Savasana is usually the last step of a yoga class where you take time to relax your body and mind. As a yogi, you should never ignore savasana. This is because relaxation is an important part of yoga, which brings balance to your body. Furthermore, you can distract the class if you walk out during savasana.

- *Don't push yourself too hard*

There is no denying how beneficial yoga is when you do it right. However, you should never push yourself too hard by trying to do poses you can't. This is because you might end up injuring yourself, which will definitely not help you attain the benefits you are looking for. What you should do is practice poses the best way you can, without you straining yourself. Then you can learn to perfect them as you go on.

- *Don't drink water 30 minutes after yoga*

When you do yoga, you usually build up some fire in you known as ushna. When you drink water immediately or anywhere, in the first 30 minutes after a yoga session, you normally cool yourself and bring the ushna down; that process normally comes with side effects. Some of these side effects include a build- up of excess mucus, allergies and colds. That is why you should avoid drinking water 30 minutes after a yoga workout.

- *Don't do vigorous jobs after yoga*

Yoga is usually a relaxing type of exercise. It is meant to relax your body and your mind so when you do vigorous jobs after a yoga class, you usually beat the purpose of a yoga class. In addition, it is a step backward when you do yoga. You should instead focus on relaxing your body after a yoga class.

You are now ready to start yoga. The chapter below is going to take you through some of the basic yoga poses that you may do in your class or that you can do in the comfort of your home.

Buy the Audio version of this book by clicking here:
  https://itunes.apple.com/us/audiobook/
yoga-for-beginners-your-guide-to-master-yoga-poses/
id1441152740

Section 3: Basic Yoga Poses

Before continue, please refer to your audiobook companion PDF that comes free with your purchase of this audiobook to see and learn all the Yoga poses, explained with images.

The moment you have been waiting for is finally here. You are now going to learn about some basic yoga poses that you can do at home or under supervision at a studio. The poses you are about to learn are generally good at strengthening your body and calming your mind. Each pose will come with a brief description of its benefits and how you can perform it.

Mountain Pose

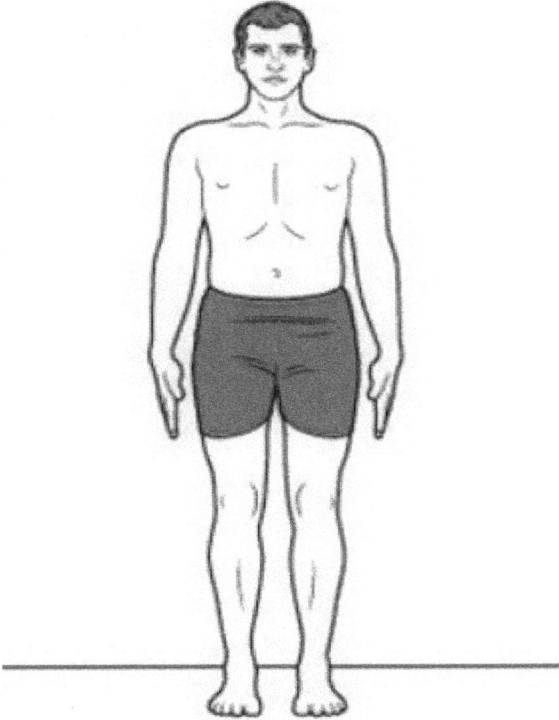

As a beginner, mountain pose may not seem like much of a pose to you but trust me it is very effective. If you practice this pose correctly, the muscles in your body especially your lower body will all be engaged. This pose is usually the blueprint that all other poses are found on and it is good at promoting balance and directing your attention to the present.

How to do it

1. Start by standing with your feet together and your arms at your sides.

2. Ground your feet, by pressing down all your toes.

3. Now engage your quadriceps as you lift up your kneecaps through your inner thighs.

4. Slowly breathe in and as you do, lengthen through your torso and raise your hands up and out. Breathe out as you slowly move your shoulder blades away from your head and to the back of your waist. Your arms should be back to your sides.

5. Hold on to that position for 5-10 breaths

Child's Pose (Balasana)

One of the best resting poses that you can perform as a beginner is the child's pose. Child's pose is regarded as a reset exercise, as it relaxes your nervous system which calms your body down to a state of rest. It is also good at relieving your back pains as it takes cares of the lengthening space that is in between each of your vertebrae.

The best time to perform child's pose is when you feel fatigued. But you can also use it when you need some stress relief, a mental break or a breather from an activity that you are doing.

How to do it

1. Start on all fours with your toes tacked under. Bring your feet and knees together.
2. Sit back on your heels, inhale and then exhale as you stretch your arms forward bringing your torso down to the point that you can rest your forehead on the mat/blanket/pillow.
3. Breathe deeply and hold on to this position for as long as you can.

Downward Facing Dog (Adho Mukha Svanansana)

The downward facing dog pose is a classic pose that is known to stretch your hamstrings, open your shoulders and lengthen your spine. It is used in most yoga practices for the sole purpose of stretching, as it is good at stretching and strengthening your entire body. However, that's not all, this posture also creates a calming effect that gets you relaxed and centered.

How to do it

1. Get into an all fours position with your wrist under your shoulders, your knees under your hips and toes tucked. Walk your hands one palm's length forward.

2. Lift your hips off the floor and slightly bring them towards your heels. Your body should create a V-shape position. If you are not that flexible or your hamstrings are tight just bend your knees to take your weight back to the legs.
3. Press into your hands and rotate your inner elbows towards each other. Keep the torso moving back towards your thighs while engaging your legs.
4. Hold on to that position for 5-8 breaths before going to your original position to rest.

Cat/Cow Pose (Marjaryasana To Bitilasana)

The cat/cow pose is actually a combination of two postures, which are done together with the aim of flexing your spine in a gentle way. As a beginner, this movement will give you a feeling of what the combination of breath and movement is like. It will also warm your back, help address mobility and work on your core without the extra stress on your shoulders and on your wrists.

How to do it

1. Start by kneeling down with your hands on the floor. Create a dog like position. Your spine should be neutral and your abs engaged.
2. Slowly breathe in and then out. As you breathe out, round your spine up in the direction of the ceiling. Release your neck as you tuck your chin towards your chest.
3. Breathe in a while relaxing your abs and then arch your back. Hold on to that position for 5-10 breaths.
4. Slowly lift your head up to go back to your starting position.

Plank

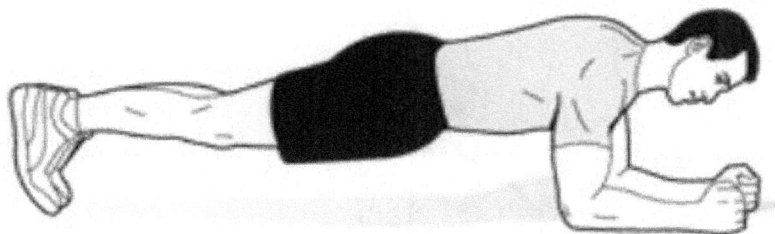

Plank is considered one of the best full body workouts in yoga. The plank mainly teaches you how to use your breath to help you stay in challenging positions. Holding on to a plank position makes you feel like your shoulders and arms are starting to burn. It also strengthens your core and makes your legs stronger. Basically it is a good pose for promoting stability and strengthening your abdominals.

How to do it

1. Start by getting in a downward facing dog position.
2. Slightly walk your hands forward so your shoulders are set over your wrists.
3. Stretch your heels back and lengthen your head forward.
4. Put your elbows down to form a straight line of energy from your feet to your head.
5. Engage your lower abdominals, pull your ribs together and deeply breathe for 8-10 breaths before you rest.

Tree Pose (Vriksasana)

Tree pose imitates the strong foundation of a tree and how easy its branches take control when it's windy. As a beginner, this fantastic standing balance pose will help you improve your concentration, clarity and ability to balance through strengthening your outer hips and the arches of your feet.

How to do it

1. Start in a mountain pose.
2. Slowly bend your left knee and bring it into your right leg's upper inner thigh. You can assist your left foot to get there with your hands. If you are not flexible enough to do that, you can bring your foot to the shin below your foot instead of your

upper inner thigh.

3. Press into your standing foot as you engage your abdominals and relax your shoulders.

4. Put your hands together as if you are praying. Find a spot and gaze at it. Hold on to your position for 8-10 breaths. Switch sides and repeat the process.

Triangle Pose (Trikonasana)

The triangle pose is usually a bit challenging but it is as beneficial as it is challenging. This pose normally helps you increase your flexibility. It also promotes balance and feelings of calmness that comes from your inner thighs and hamstrings stretch.

How to do it

1. Start by standing with your feet hip-distance apart with your arms on your sides.
2. Inhale and exhale as you softly draw your attention inwards.
3. Step apart to create a space between your legs that is 4-5 feet apart.
4. Turn your right foot to 90 degrees.
5. Turn your left foot inwards to create a 45 degrees angle at the back of your toes.
6. Engage your abdominals and quadriceps as you switch to the side that is over your right leg.
7. Move your right hand from your sides and place them down

on your knee/shin or ankle then lift your left arm towards the ceiling.

8. Turn your head and gaze up towards your top hand. Hold for 5-8 breaths.
9. Switch sides and repeat.

Corpse Pose (Shavasana)

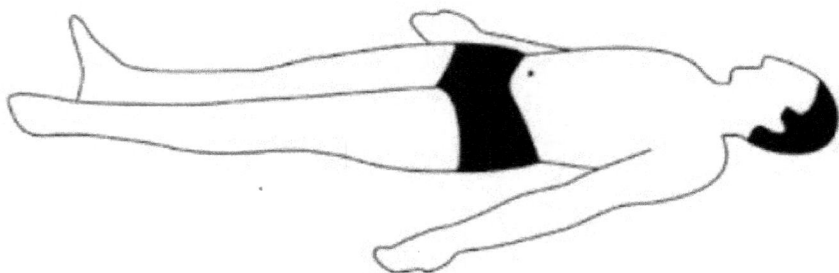

As a beginner, the corpse pose might seem like a simple posture of lying down but don't let its simplicity fool you. It is the best meditative posture in any yoga practice. The corpse pose normally relieves stress, calms your mind and induces you into a state of relaxation. It is usually practiced at the end of a yoga practice which also gives you time to enjoy the benefits of yoga.

How to do it

1. Start by lying down on your back.
2. Place your arms alongside your torso. They should be slightly separated with the palms facing up.
3. Close your eyes and relax.
4. Hold the pose for 1-10 minutes.

Easy Pose (Sukhasana)

The easy pose is a great way of building your foundation of breathing and meditation exercises. As a beginner, this posture will help you strengthen your back as well as stretch your ankles and knees. It will also open your hips and help bring your spine into the right alignment, which automatically reduces stress and anxiety.

How to do it

1. Sit up straight with legs extended in front of you.
2. Gently bend your legs and place both of your feet beneath the opposite knee.
3. Fold your legs towards your torso and place your palms

together facing down on your knees.

4. Relax your feet and thighs and gaze in a spot in front of you.

5. Hold that position for as long as you wish then release and change the cross of your legs.

Warrior I (Virabhadrasana I)

The warrior I pose is good at building your strength and stamina. When you perform it, it stretches your front body, which includes hip flexors, quads and psoas while also strengthening your core, buttocks, hips and legs. As a beginner, this pose will increase your balance and concentration.

How to do it

1. Start by getting in the mountain pose. Inhale and then exhale as you move your left foot back about 4 feet to get into a lunge position. Your right ankle should be over your right knee.
2. Turn your left foot to form a 90-degree angle and then raise your arms straight overhead.

3. Enlarge your chest and pull your shoulders back. Slowly lower down to the floor with your arms lifted up and breathe. Return to the original position and repeat with the opposite leg.

Warrior II (Virabhadrasana II)

The warrior II is similar to warrior I, since you get the same quad-strength benefit but with a slight difference in performance. When performing warrior II you usually rotate your upper body to the sides instead of facing forward as you do in warrior I. That slight difference increases your flexibility by opening up your hip flexor muscles.

How to do it

1. Start by standing in the mountain pose and then slowly place your feet apart.
2. Gently turn your right toes to 90 degrees and your left toes to 45 degrees.
3. Bend your right knee forward until it is right over your right ankle. Your torso should remain even between your hips.

4. Raise your arms up and then turn the right arm in front of you and left the arm behind you.
5. Gaze over your right arm for 8-10 breaths. Return to the starting point, exchange the legs and repeat.

Crescent Lunge

Crescent lunge is a pose that offers you a deep stretch for your legs, groin and hip flexors. It also helps you open your front body including your shoulders and chest. As a beginner, crescent lunge will help you practice balancing and will strengthen your butt, hips and thighs.

How to do it

1. Start in a standing position. Slowly start stepping back with your left foot to create a position where your feet are leg's height apart.
2. Bend your right knee to 90 degrees and then lift both your arms straight overhead.
3. Lengthen the back leg while reaching up as you relax your shoulders. Hold that position for 30 seconds then switch sides

and repeat.

Chair Pose (Utkatasana)

This standing pose is usually good at building strength and stamina. As a beginner, you can expect your shins and Achilles tendons to be stretched when doing this pose. You can also expect your ankles and thighs to be strengthened while your back hips and shoulders are toned.

How to do it

1. Start in the mountain pose with your feet together. A beginner like you can start with your feet hip distance to reduce the intensity of the pose.
2. Breathe in a while raising your arms overhead. Now breathe out as you bend your knees to a point where your thighs are parallel to the floor.

3. Lower your hips as if there is a chair you are sitting on.
4. Shift your weight to your heels as you lengthen up your torso.
5. Gaze directly forward and then hold on to that position for about one minute.

Half Spinal Twist (Ardha Matsyendrasana)

This twist is very good for your spine. Basically it increases your spine's elasticity, which is suitable for tension release. The pose also opens up your chest increasing the oxygen supply in your lungs.

How to do it

1. Start by sitting down with your legs stretched in front.
2. Gently bend your right leg and rest its heel beside your left hip.
3. Rest your right hand on your left knee and the left hand behind you. Gently twist your waist, neck and shoulders to the left as you look over your left shoulder.
4. Hold that position as you take long breaths for 1-5 minutes.
5. To get out of this position, you should release your left hand first and then release your waist, chest and neck to sit up straight. Switch sides and repeat.

Lunge (Anjaneyasana)

If you have tight hips then this is the yoga pose for you. It is an amazing hip opener but that is not all it does. It is also good at stretching your quadriceps and gluteus muscles, which improve your concentration, balance and core awareness.

How to do it

1. Start in a downward facing dog position. Exhale as you step your right foot forward resting it besides your right thumb.
2. Gently lower your left knee towards the floor. Inhale and raise your torso while at the same time raising your arms over your head with your palms facing each other.
3. Breathe out as you move your hips forward and down until

you feel your psoas and the front of your left leg stretching.

4. Engage your core muscles as you lengthen your lower back. Slowly start reaching back with your thumbs. Gaze upwards and hold on to that position for 1-5 minutes. Switch sides and repeat.

5. To exit the pose, slowly place your hands on the floor and step back into a downward facing dog pose.

Pigeon Pose

The pigeon pose is amazing owing to its many benefits. Some of these benefits include how it lengthens your hip flexor and increases the external range of femur motion in your hip socket. It also stretches you and prepares you for seated postures and backbends.

How to do it

1. Start in a downward dog position.
2. Lift up your left leg and slide it forward up to the back of your right wrist.
3. Straighten your right leg and slowly let the front of your thigh rest on the floor then lower the right buttocks to the floor.
4. Extend your hands forward resting them on either side of your legs. Lay your torso on the left leg.
5. Hold this position for 4-5 breaths.
6. Switch sides and repeat.

Supine Spinal Twist (Supta Matsyendrasana)

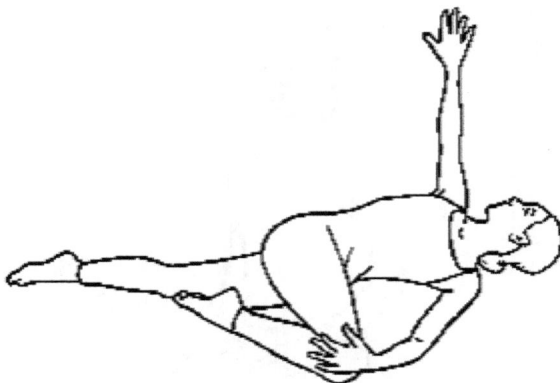

If you are in yoga for strength and stress relief you are going to love supine spinal twist. This pose normally stretches your hamstrings and knees, which strengthens your legs. It also stretches your spine, back muscles and stimulates your intestines, urinary bladder, abdominal organs and kidneys, which all release stress.

How to do it

1. Start by lying down on your back with your legs stretched in front.
2. Bend your knees and rotate your hips to the right side, stretch your right leg and cross your other knee over to the right side.
3. Stretch your left arm out onto the left side as you rest your right hand on your left knee.
4. Gently turn your head to the left. Hold onto that pose for 30 seconds to 1 minute.
5. Breathe out as you release the pose. Switch sides and repeat.

Hero (Virasana)

As a beginner, this pose will teach you how to rotate your inner thigh as it reduces the tightness in your legs. The hero pose is good because it increases your flexibility in the thighs, ankles and knees when it stretches them. A part from that, it can improve your posture and relieve you from asthma.

How to do it

1. Start on all fours with your knees closer together and your feet hip width apart. Your hips should be directly under your hips.
2. Lower your hips slowly until you are sitting on your heels. (This can be difficult for you at first so you can place a cushion between your heels and sit on it). As you sit, your toes should point back.
3. Sit upright and then lengthen your tailbone to the floor with your hands laid on your thighs.

4. Hold on to that pose for 5-10 breaths as you gaze downwards.

Boat Pose

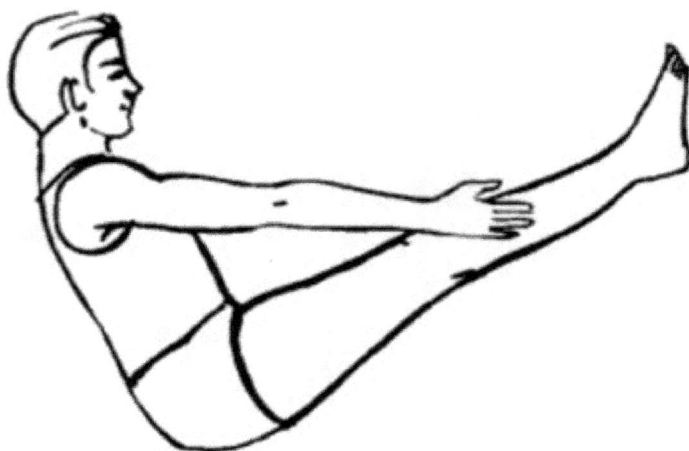

The boat pose usually requires you to be stable. As a beginner, this pose will stimulate your abdominal organs and improve your digestion. It will also challenge your hip flexors, spine and abdomen, which strengthen your body's core. Lastly, it will help you in maintaining your metabolism and in releasing stress.

How to do it

1. Begin in a sitting position with your legs stretched forward and your hands are resting behind your hips.
2. Inhale as you strengthen your arms and then exhale and slowly lift your feet off the mat by bending your knees. The thighs should be 45-50 degrees to the floor. If you can, straighten your knees and raise them high to a point that your toes are at the level of your eyes. As a beginner, just let your knees bent.
3. Stretch your hands alongside your legs. They should be

parallel to each other.

4. Hold on to that position for 1-5 minutes.

Dolphin

The dolphin pose is one of the popular poses good at strengthening and stretching your legs, upper back, arms and shoulders. However, it does not just strengthen, it also increases flexibility in your arches, calves, hamstrings and spine.

How to do it

1. Begin on all fours position with your wrist under your shoulders and your knees under your hips.
2. Gently lower your elbows to rest on the mat under your shoulders. Your forearms should be parallel to each other and your weight distributed evenly on your forearms.
3. Get your knees off the floor and let your pelvis reach up towards the ceiling. Bring your buttocks toward the wall behind you.
4. Broaden your shoulders, bend your knees and lengthen your spine.
5. Gently straighten your legs to create an 'A' shape with your

body. If your upper back starts to round, slightly bend your knees and your spine will be straight.

6. Relax your head and gaze between your legs.

7. Hold onto that position for 5-25 breaths.

Bridge (Setu Bandha Sarvangasana)

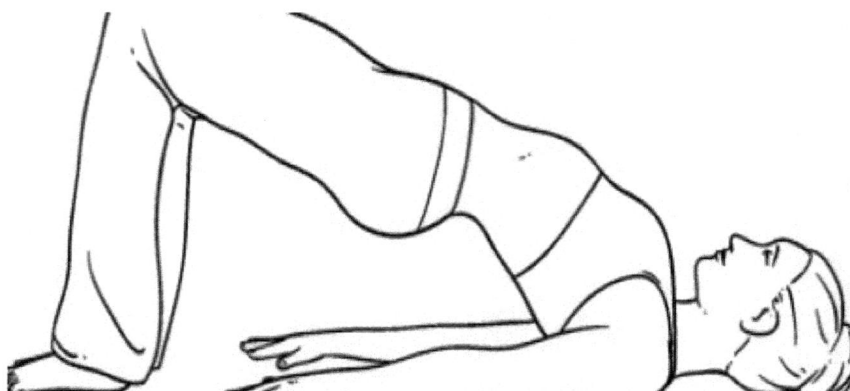

The Bridge is an amazing pose when it comes to stretching your front body and strengthening your back body. Normally, it stretches your neck and spine and opens up your chest. These two factors help your mind to calm down and your anxiety to go away.

How to do it

1. Start by laying down with your face up, arms on your sides and feet flat on the floor. Your feet should be hip-width apart.
2. Press your feet firmly and use that strength to lift your behind up off the floor.
3. Interlock your hands and then press your fists down to the floor. This will automatically open up your chest.
4. Engage your hamstrings by slowly dragging your heels towards your shoulders. Hold on to that posture for 8-10 breaths. Lower your hips and repeat the whole process 2 times.

Bound Angle (Baddha Konasana)

The bound angle pose is a seated yoga posture, which is good at stretching your inner thighs, knees, groin and hips. It is also good at improving the circulation of your blood throughout your entire body. If you are a woman, it can soothe your menstrual discomfort as well as help you to have a smooth childbirth when you are Pregnant.

How to do it

1. Start in a normal seated position with your hands on the sides as palms rest on the mat. Your legs should be stretched in front of you.
2. Bring your heels in towards your pelvis as you bend your knees. Bring your soles together and let them press against each other as you drop both of your knees open.

3. Use your hands to press down your feet. Meanwhile press down your feet firmly together.

4. Lengthen your spine to sit upright. Gaze forward and hold to that pose for 1-5 minutes.

Standing Forward Bend (Uttanasana)

The standing forward bend has been known to have some amazing effects on your body. For instance, it improves the blood circulation in your head when you bend your head down. That enables the cells in your head to be re-energized with the amount of oxygen supplied to it. It also stretches your hamstrings, which releases some stress in your muscles and calms you down.

How to do it

1. Start by standing up with your feet together.
2. Soften your knees as you gently bend forward folding your torso.
3. Let your hands rest on the ground or next to your feet. Breathe

in and out, as you broaden your chest to lengthen your spine. Feel the fold from your hipbone. Make sure you don't feel the fold from your lower back (if you do, then you are doing something wrong)

4. If you don't feel a stretch in your hamstrings gently stretch your knees more.

5. With your head bent towards the floor gaze through your legs and hold on to that position for 30 seconds – 5 minutes.

Cobra (Bhujangasana)

The cobra pose helps you to prepare for advance backbend poses as it is a simple backbend pose. By performing this pose, your spine flexibility will be increased and your digestion improved, as it stimulates your abdominal organs. It is also good at helping you relax when you are fatigued.

How to do it

1. Start by lying face down on your yoga mat. Your legs should be extended behind you with your toes pointing away from you.
2. Bring your hands to your chest and press down from your feet to your pubic bone.
3. Engage your back and gluteal muscles as you straighten your arms and lift your head and chest off the mat.
4. Deepen the stretch by trying to lift your head further up. Now gaze upwards and hold on to that pose for 1-5 minutes.

Legs up the Wall (Viparita karani)

The Viparita Karani has a couple of benefits to your body. For starters, it helps in blood circulation especially in your upper body area. Secondly, its leg up position helps stretch your back from the heel all the way up to your upper back. Thirdly, if you are a woman you will be happy to know it can relieve the symptoms of menstruation as it massages your reproductive organs.

How to do it

1. As a beginner, you can use a prop like a pillow to perform this pose. If you are using a prop, start by placing the pillow under your lower back with your left side against the wall.
2. Slowly turn your body to the left as you bring your legs up the wall; use your hands for balance.
3. Let your upper body rest on the floor as you rest your

shoulders. Your arms should be rested on the sides.

4. Relax your buttocks area and close your eyes. Hold that position for 5-10 minutes, as you breathe with awareness. Once done, push yourself away from the wall and slide your legs to the right side.

Plow

The plow yoga pose is a bend pose that is known for its ability to alleviate back pain, improve blood circulation, increase your spine's flexibility and relieve you of stress as it energizes your body.

How to do it

1. Start by lying face up on the floor with your arms on your sides.
2. Inhale as you engage your core to lift your feet off the ground stretching them backward to a 90-degree angle. Use your hands to support your lower back and hips when stretching your legs.
3. Continue stretching your feet backward with the help of your hands of course until the feet rest behind you. Gently remove your arms from your hips and interlock them together before stretching them forward. Press the hands down as you lift your thighs and hips higher.
4. Hold on to that posture for 1-5 minutes.

Four-Limbed Staff Pose (Chaturanga)

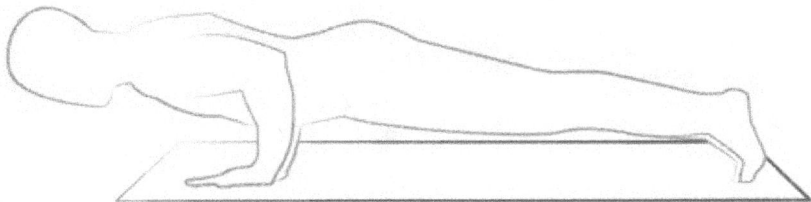

The four-limbed staff pose is good at preparing you as a beginner for advanced arm balancing poses. In this pose, your wrist and arms will be strengthened and your abdomen toned.

How to do it

1. Start from a plank pose.
2. Breathe out as you lower your legs and torso to within an inch or two from the floor. As a beginner, you might not be able to perform the pose as it is required so you are allowed to lower your knees to the ground.
3. Let your arms and legs support you as you gaze forward.
4. Hold that position for 1-2 minutes.

Warrior III Pose (Virabhadra)

One of the best postures when it comes to improving balance and coordination is warrior III pose. This pose usually tones your abdomen muscles, strengthens your legs and ankles and stretches your hamstrings, shoulders and chest, which release you from stress and calms down your body.

How to do it

1. Begin in the mountain pose with your feet hip-distance apart.
2. Breathe in and stretch your arms over your head. As you breathe out, start to slowly extend your left leg straight behind you. Shift your weight to your right leg.
3. Straighten the left leg as you engage your right leg quadriceps to help it remain strong to support your body.
4. Let your neck relax in a neutral position as you gaze downwards. Stay in this position for 5-10 breaths. Switch sides and repeat.
5. Come out the position by bringing your left foot back on the ground and then raise your upper body up.

King Dancer Pose

For those who lack focus and concentration, king dancer pose is what you need. This is because it teaches you how to calmly balance which heightens your focus. Its posture also helps you develop better flexibility in your hamstring, shoulders and spine.

How to do it

1. Start by standing upright with your feet shoulder-width apart.
2. Slowly shift your weight to the right foot as you lift your left foot off the ground and towards your back.
3. Extend your left arm backward and support your left foot by holding it just above the ankle. Your right arm should be pointed straight forward.
4. Use your left arm to lift your left leg higher as the knees bend to accommodate the pull. Your toes should be almost at the

same length with your head.

5. Hold on to that position for 5-10 breaths.
6. Switch legs and repeat.

Seated Forward Bend (Paschimottanasana)

Seated forward bend is an important pose to be incorporated into yoga practice because it helps you stretch your hamstrings and your lower and upper back. The stretch in this pose helps in improving your digestion, calming your brain, relieving stress off your muscles and in soothing anxiety and headaches.

How to do it

1. Begin in a seated position with your legs together. Your hands should be on your hips.
2. Gently lift up your chest and start moving forward towards your feet from your waist up. Engage your lower abdominals as you move forward. Go as low as you can and then stop, release your neck and your head and hold on to that position for 8-10 breaths.

Now that you have seen the basic yoga poses it's time for you to now take a look at the yoga routines you can follow as a beginner. Check this out in the next chapter.

Buy the Audio version of this book by clicking here:

https://itunes.apple.com/us/audiobook/
yoga-for-beginners-your-guide-to-master-yoga-poses/
id1441152740

Section 4: Basic Yoga Routines

Before continue, please refer to your audiobook companion PDF that comes free with your purchase of this audiobook to see and learn all the Yoga poses, explained with images.

The moment you have been waiting for is finally here. In this chapter, you will learn 5 yoga routines that you can follow as a beginner. These basic yoga routines are good for helping you kick off your yoga journey so carefully read how to do each one of them before trying them out.

Here are the 5 yoga routines.

The fact is that it is quite challenging to try to avoid stress; however, you can learn how to manage it in a healthy way. The below routine will help you release some of your stress.

Warm-Up Poses

1. Easy Pose (Sukhasana)

This meditative pose is brilliant to start with when on a stress relief routine. It is ideal to begin with because it gives you time to meditate and think about why you are doing what you are doing in the first place. It also gives you time to think about what you are hoping to accomplish on the mat. Do the easy pose for 1 minute.

1. **Standing Side Body Stretch (Ardha Chandrasana Variation)**

Sometimes when you are stressed, all you need is to breathe and that is what your second yoga pose is about; getting a breather. This yoga pose normally stretches your upper body and expands your lungs. The expansion of your lungs brings more oxygen in your body, which drives stress out from your cells and improves your oxygen circulation.

But how do you perform it? This is how:

1. Begin in the mountain pose with your legs together. Your core should be engaged, shoulders relaxed and chest raised.
2. Stretch your arms forward and interlace your fingers.
3. Raise your arms up and over to your right side. Keep the arms straight with the biceps closely by your ears. Hold that position for 30-60 seconds.
4. Come back to the middle and then repeat the process but this

time raise your arms over to the left side.

Stress Free Yoga Poses

1. Revolved Side Angle Pose (Parivritta Parsvakonasana)

The above poses have just warmed you up and the next step is for you to do some stress relief yoga exercises. The revolved side angle pose is the perfect exercise to start with because its diaphragmatic breathing will help you re-energize yourself and snap out of your lethargic slump.

Here is how to do it:

1. Start by standing upright on your knees.
2. Inhale and as you exhale take your right foot off the ground and step it forward into a 90-degree angle. Place your hands on your hips.
3. Lean your upper body towards your right leg and twist your upper body towards your right side
4. Rest your left elbow on your right knee and create a prayer

posture with your hands.

5. Gently get your left knee off the ground and stretch it towards your back. Your heel should be open.

6. Now break the prayer posture by placing your left arm on the floor just outside your right leg and raising your right arm up as you gaze to the ceiling.

7. Stay in that position for 3-5 long breaths.

1. King Dancer Pose (Natarajasana)

The dance pose is good for stretching your hips abs, quads, shoulders and chest, which helps your body release some muscle stress. Hold on to it for 1 minute, switch legs and repeat the process for another 1 minute.

1. Cow Pose (Bitilasana)

The cow pose is an amazing stress relief pose and this is because it gently massages your belly organs and your spine. It also stretches your neck and your torso, which are all good stress relievers.

This is how you can perform it.

1. Start on all fours with your knees directly under your hips and your hands directly under your shoulders.
2. Slowly lift your tailbone so that your back can curve downwards. You should not force your back to go down instead just let the downward curve happen naturally.
3. Pick a spot in front of you where you can gaze as you breathe gently for 30 seconds to 1 minute.

1. Cat Pose (Marjaryasana)

The cat pose is similar to the cow pose. They all help in massaging your spine and belly organs. The only extra special thing that the cow pose has is its ability to relax your back and improve your blood circulation. That helps in reducing stress, which is why the two poses are good when they follow each other.

Here is how to do a cat pose:

1. Start on an all fours position like the cow pose did but this time don't let your back curve downwards instead round your spine up towards the roof.
2. Gently let your head fall downwards and gaze on the floor for 30 seconds – 1 minute.

1. Supported Bridge Poses (Setu Bandha Sarvangasana)

The supported bridge pose is an amazing exercise for opening up your heart, which helps you get rid of all the stress that hangs around your chest area.

So how is it done? This exercise is similar to the bridge pose you learnt in the previous chapter. The only difference is that in this method you are going to use a prop for support. One of the best props to use here is a block. So perform it like a normal bridge but this time place blocks under your lumbar and sacrum.

Maintain this position for 1 minute.

Congratulations you have completed the circuit now let us cool down.

Cool Down Poses

1. **Child's Pose (Baasana)**

Ending your yoga session with a child's pose is a perfect way of relaxing your body and mind. This pose helps you get into a deep state of relaxation. In this state, you usually bask on the benefits of being relieved from stress and that creates a calming and satisfying feeling.

Yoga Routine For Strength

If you are looking to build strength, then this is the routine for you.

Warm-Up

Let us get started with some warm-up poses you can do

1. Mountain Pose

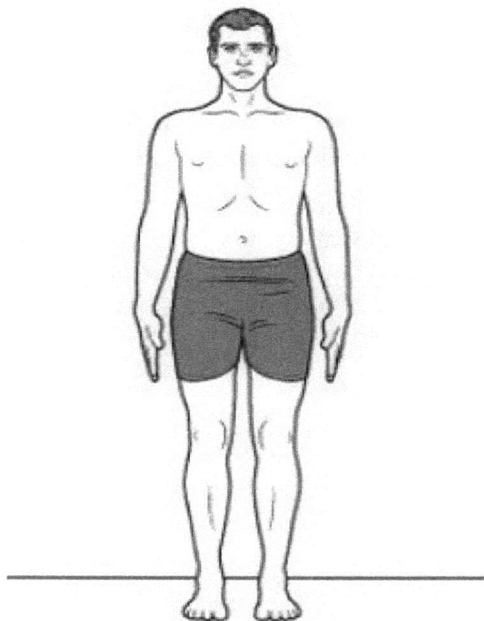

The mountain pose is the perfect pose to start with when doing strength yoga routines because it focuses on warming up your whole body. In addition, it improves your digestion, respiration as well as leaves you are feeling motivated.

Perform it as you saw in the previous chapter and then hold the position for 2 minutes.

1. Standing forward bend to flat back

Your warm-up session becomes more effective when you do the standing forward bend to flat back. These poses are usually good because they stretch your calves and hamstrings reliving them of any stress. They also strengthen your knees and thighs, which is nice because you are going to need those organs to be fit when you start doing strength poses.

Here is how to do standing forward bend to flat back.

1. **Start by doing the standing forward bend pose.** Begin in the mountain pose.
2. Bend your knees and fold your upper body over your legs. Stretch your arms downwards to rest next to your feet. Extend your chest and gaze forward.
3. Inhale, exhale and as you exhale, press both of your legs in order for them to be straight. Hold on to that position for 1 minute and let your inner legs activate as your hamstrings stretch.

4. **Move to a flat back pose.** Right from the standing forward bend raise your upper body up. Bring your spine flat and your shoulders back.

5. Bend your knees slightly and then step back with your left knee to go to a lunge position. Hold on to that position for 1 minute.

Strength Poses

Let us now look at some poses to build your strength:

1. Dolphin Push-Ups

Now that your muscles are all warmed up, you are ready to start building body strength and the first pose that you are going to do is a dolphin push up. The dolphin push up is a muscle-pumping pose, which helps you build strength in your upper body and more specifically in your chest and arm area without it spraining your wrist.

Here is how to perform it:

1. Start on all fours to get to the pose. Your knees should be under your butt and wrist under your shoulders.
2. Gently lift your knees off the ground and raise your butt area towards the ceiling to create a 'V' shape.
3. Put your elbows down on the ground and hook your hands together.

4. Slowly walk your legs backward until you form a straight line from your heels up to your head.
5. Start doing the push-ups. Exhale as you lift your hips up into a downward facing dog and then inhale as you go back to the plank position.
6. Repeat the whole process for 10 inhales and exhales.

1. Bridge poses (setu Bandha Sarvangasana)

The Bridge Pose with leg lift has the same benefits that a bridge pose has with one of the outstanding ones being its ability to strengthen your core muscles. In addition, it revitalizes your legs and increases your energy.

Here is how to perform it:

1. Lie on your back, knees bent, your feet on the floor, hip width and arms at your side with palms down.
2. Press your arms and feet firmly on the floor and engage your core muscles to lift your hips towards the ceiling.
3. Slowly stretch your right leg up towards the ceiling. Hold for 2 breaths and then lower it to the ground.
4. Lift your left leg upwards, hold for 2-5 breaths and then lower to the ground.

5. Repeat the whole process 5 times.

Plank

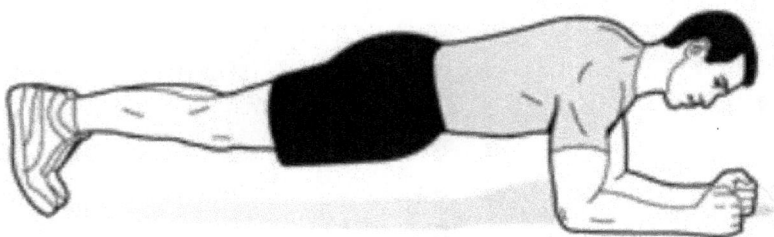

The plank pose is quite beneficial to your body with the most notable ones being how it tones your buttocks and how it improves your endurance. However, those are not the benefits that have landed it into this list. What has is how good it is when it comes to increasing your strength. This pose normally strengthens your spinal muscles, neck muscles, triceps, wrist and hands muscles. That is why it is a great yoga pose to perform in this category.

You can perform it as you were taught in the previous chapter and then hold it for 30 seconds to 1 hour. Do 3 reps.

1. Tree Pose

The tree pose is popularly known for its ability to improve balance, focus and concentration but this one-legged standing pose does more than that to your body. One of the extra things it does is to strengthen your lower body muscles and more specifically your legs.

Perform it as you learned in the previous chapter for 30 seconds- 1 minute and then do 3 reps.

1. Chair Pose (Utkatasana)

The awkward chair pose is amazing when it comes to strengthening your thighs so it is the next pose that you are going to perform. The last chapter taught you how to perform it so you are going to follow those instructions only this time you are going to hold on to the position for longer. Hold for 1 minute and do 2 reps.

1. Standing Split Pose (Urdha Prasarita Eka Padasana)

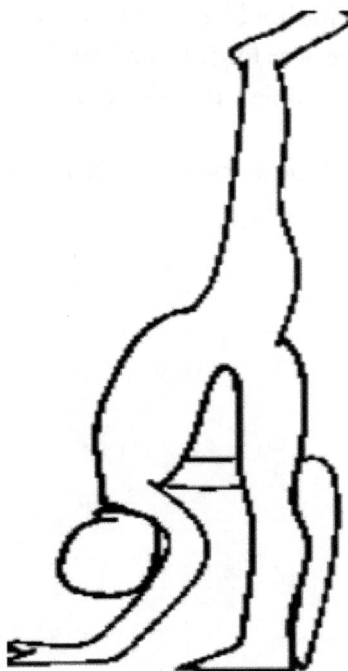

Standing split pose is challenging than the poses you have just seen. That said, it is very beneficial and that is why it is our 6th pose. The standing split basically stretches all the muscles in your legs. It also strengthens a couple of muscles in your legs, which include your ankles, knees and thighs.

Here is how you do it:

1. From the mountain pose, pivot at your hips and come into a forward fold. Your fingertips should be able to touch the mat/ ground.

2. Shift your weight onto your left foot and let it be distributed

     evenly on all corners of your foot.

3. Gently breathe in as you lift your right leg towards the ceiling. Try as much as possible to keep your front pelvis parallel to the floor. Your hips should also be in line with one another.

4. Maintain that pose for 5-10 breaths.

5. Switch legs and repeat the whole process. Do 2 reps.

Repeat the strength poses twice before heading to the cool down exercise.

Cool Down Poses

1. Corpse pose

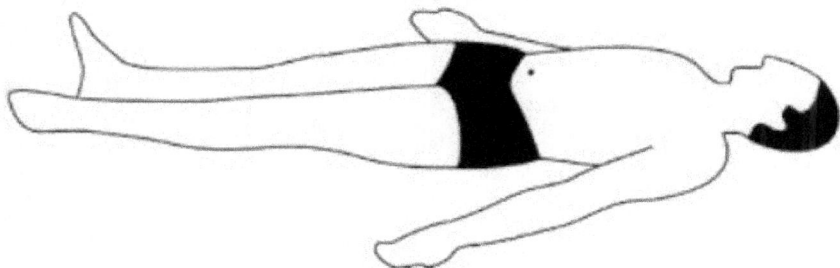

The perfect way to end your strength yoga routine is by doing the powerful relaxation pose called the corpse pose. This pose is usually great for relaxing your whole body. It calms your mind and provides a peaceful environment that you can use to relax or think about the benefits of the poses you have just done.

Perform it as you learned in the previous chapter and do it for 5-10 minutes.

Yoga Routine For Boosting Your Energy

Learn how to improve your energy by doing the following yoga routine.

Warm-Ups Poses

1. Cobra Pose

The Cobra Pose is the best yoga pose to start with when you want to boost your energy in the morning. This is because it is a great warm-up poses that increases flexibility in your spine, tones your buttocks, abdomen and shoulders and last but not least it stretches and strengthens your chest and spine. In short, it generally prepares your body for yoga workouts more specifically backbends workouts.

To perform it, just follow the directions that you were given in the previous chapter. Hold for 30 seconds- 1 minute and do 3 reps.

1. Downward Facing Dog

After the cobra pose, you should move to the downward facing dog. This pose qualifies for our second warm-up pose because it lengthens, strengthens and energizes all your muscles. It also improves the blood flow to your brain, which sharpens your focus for the rest of the exercises.

Perform it as you learned in the previous chapter. Hold for 1 minute and do 3 reps.

Energetic Yoga Poses

1. Warrior I

The first yoga pose that you must perform after the warm-up is the warrior I pose. This pose is going to help you increase your body-mind connection. That mental boost develops into inner strength and courage that results in an increase in self-confidence and body energy.

Perform the warrior I pose the same way you were taught in the previous chapter. Hold for 1 minute, switch legs and repeat the whole process. Do 3 reps.

1. Warrior II

Now that you have built a powerful inner strength, the next step is for you to do a Warrior II pose. This pose is similar to warrior I in terms of the benefits it offers but there is one unique thing about warrior II and that is its ability to dissolve tensions while still holding on to strength and energy.

In short, it helps you be energetic without you having tense muscles. To perform it, you only need to follow the instructions you were given in the previous chapter of how to perform it only this time hold the position for 2 minutes. Do 2 reps.

1. Spinal Flex/Camel Ride

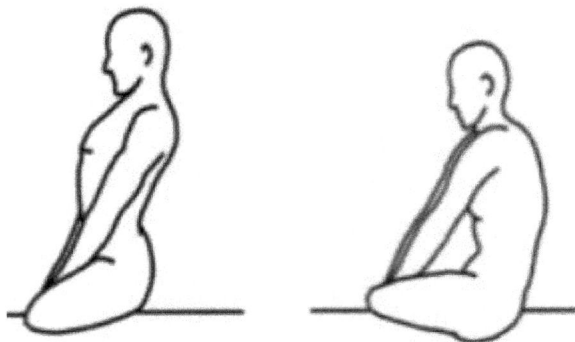

The camel ride pose is your next pose from warrior II because it helps you have a fresh circulation that flows throughout your spine, which reenergizes every system that is in your body. It also relieves your back problem, which allows you to have a boost in energy.

Here is how to do it:

1. Begin in an easy pose with your hands holding onto your shins or your calves.
2. Inhale and exhale as you round up your spin with your chin on the chest.
3. Go back to the original easy pose then go again while you increase your pace. Continue doing that for 1 minute. Do 3 reps.

1. Arm Pumps

After the camel ride pose, you should slowly transition to the arm pump pose. Arm pump pose normally increases the intensity of your energy sequence exercise by working your shoulders, lats and triceps. Its movement is what increases the energy in your body.

Here is how to perform it:

1. Come out from your seated position and kneel down with your legs together and your upper body straight up.
2. Fall back and sit down on your heels with your hands locked in front of you, palms in and knuckles out.
3. Inhale as you bring your hands up and over your head. Stop. Exhale as you bring your locked arms back to your knees. Continue this motion for 2 minutes. Do 2 reps.

1. Bow Pose

The bow pose normally stretches your entire front body while strengthening your back muscles. This pose is good for flexibility and stretching your throat, hip flexors, groin, ankles, quadriceps, abdomen and chest. The stretches and the increased flexibility is what helps in invigorating and energizing your body, mind and spirit.

Here is how to perform it:

1. Start by lying on the floor on your stomach with chin on the mat.
2. Exhale as you take your legs off the ground and stretch them towards your buttocks. Your knees should be hip-distance apart.
3. Stretch your arms backwards, reach for your legs and hold them on the outer ankle.
4. Inhale as you lift your heels further towards the ceiling; and at the same time lift your upper body off the mat and towards

the ceiling.
5. Pick a spot in front and gaze at it as you softly breathe.
6. Hold that position for 30 seconds. Release and do 3 reps.

Now repeat all the above energetic poses twice.

Cool Down Poses

Let us now look at poses you can do to cool down.

Legs up the wall

Now you need to finish your energy yoga poses with a pose that can relax you. One such pose is the legs up the wall pose. This pose is usually a restorative pose, which allows your body and mind to relieve stress, tension and relax.

You were taught how to practice this pose so just follow those instructions and do it. Hold it for 5 minutes.

Yoga Routine For Improving Sleep

Get a good night sleep with this yoga routine.

Warm-ups

1. Cat-cow stretch

The best way to start your yoga practice for better sleep is by doing a cat-cow stretch warm-up. This pose is ideal for a warm-up because it releases tension in your shoulders, torso and back. It is also good for quieting a busy mind, which is something that you need when preparing to sleep.

Perform this pose as you learned in the previous chapter. Do 2 reps of 1 minute each.

1. Child's pose

From cat-cow pose, head straight onto the child's pose. The child's pose is also known as the resting pose because it is a therapeutic posture that relieves your body of stress and brings calmness to your brain.

Perform as illustrated in the previous chapter. Do 2 reps of 2 minutes each.

Sleep Yoga Poses

1. Standing Forward Bend (*Uttanasana*)

Standing forward bend is a great pose to do when you are about to sleep. This is because it eases tensions in your hips and creates a sense of ease and calmness in your mind and body which is exactly what you need to get a good night sleep.

Follow the instructions you got from the previous chapter to perform this pose. Do 2 reps of 1 minute each.

1. Seated Forward Fold

After standing forward bend, go straight to a seated forward fold. This pose normally works on your brain by calming it and relieving it of any stress. It also stretches your hamstrings, shoulders and spine, which gets you into an even deeper state of relaxation that is good for sleeping.

Perform this pose as instructed in the previous chapter. Do 2 reps of 2 minute each.

1. **Hero Pose**

Hero pose is a transformational posture that transforms your fatigued feet, ankles, thighs and hips to body organs that are relaxed and stress-free. This pose facilitates better sleep by relaxing your body parts.

Perform this pose exactly as it was explained in the previous chapter. Do 2 reps of 2 minutes each.

1. Supine Spinal Twist (Supta Matsyendrasana)

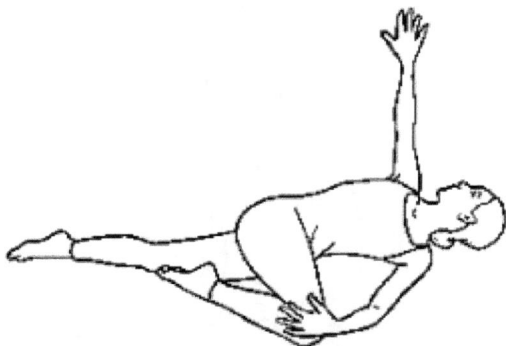

The Supine Spinal Twist is a great pose to follow the hero pose. This is because it stretches your legs more especially your hamstrings; which relieves some stress from you and leaves you feeling calm and ready for deep sleep.

Check out how to perform it in the previous chapter. Do 2 reps of 2 minutes each.

1. Happy Baby (Ananda Balasana)

The tension in your groin and hips can give you sleepless nights and that's why it is important to deal with those two areas when you want to have a better sleep. The best pose to do is the happy baby pose. This pose normally provides you with a gentle stretch to your low back, inner groin and hips. The stretches are what ease your tensions and give your body a relaxing feeling that helps you have a deep and fulfilling sleep.

Here is how to perform it:

1. Begin by lying down on the floor facing up.
2. Exhale as you bend your knees and move them towards your belly.
3. Inhale as you hold the outsides of your feet with both your

hands.

4. Slowly open up your knees so that they are wider than your torso and then move them up in the direction of your armpits; your ankles should be over your knees.

5. Flex your heels by pushing your feet up against your hands as you firmly pull your hands down to create an opposing pose.

6. Stay in that position for 5-15 breaths. Do 3 reps.

1. Reclined Cobbler's Pose

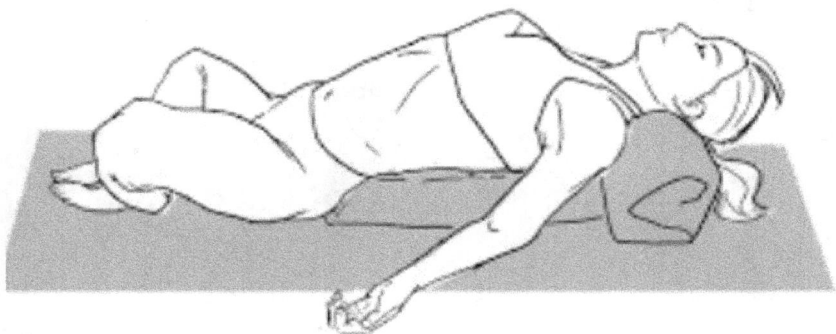

This deeply relaxing and restorative yoga pose is a good hip opener. The reason why you should do it after the happy baby is because it works on your body while providing you with calm and well-being feeling.

Here is how to do it;

1. Start by lying down on the ground face up.
2. Bend your knees and let your legs rest on the ground with your soles close together.
3. Slowly push your knees apart and then let your arms relax on either side. Your soles should be dragged towards your body for as long as you can.
4. Hold on to that position for 1 minute. Do 2 sets

Cool Down

Corpse pose

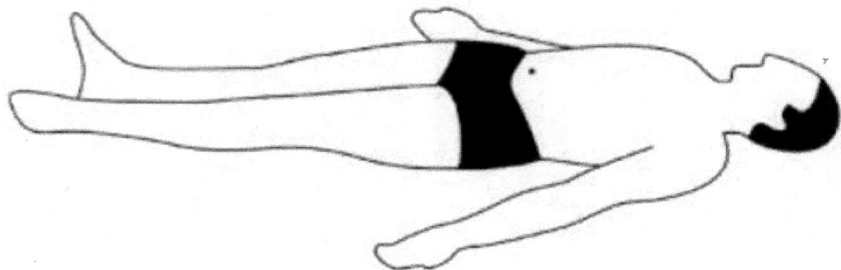

The corpse pose is the best pose to finish your yoga poses. This is because it provides you with a chance to reset your mind, which increases your level of calmness. Basically, it gives you time to unwind and let loose.

To know how to perform it, you need to visit the last chapter and again see how it's performed.

Yoga Routine For Flexibility

Yoga is one of the best exercises when it comes to enhancing flexibility. Here is a yoga routine that can help you be more flexible.

Warm-Up

1. Standing forward fold

Standing forward fold is a perfect yoga pose to warm-up on when starting a flexibility routine and this is because it deeply stretches and strengthens most of your body muscles, particularly your hamstrings and your lower back. That then prepares you for a full workout.

Here is how it is done:

1. Start in the mountain pose with your feet shoulder-width apart.
2. Slightly bend your knees to create a solid foundation and then gently lower your upper body forward.
3. Let your head hang with your arms grabbing opposite elbows.
4. Hold that position for 30 seconds – 1 minute and do 2 reps. As a beginner, you can bend your knees as you perform the

pose and only straighten your legs when you gain more flexibility. When coming back up to your standing position, do it slowly as doing it quickly can make you dizzy.

1. **Crescent pose**

For your warm-up to be efficient, you need to follow the standing forward fold pose with a crescent pose. While the standing forward fold stretches your lower body, the crescents pose works on improving your balance, stamina and posture. It does this by awakening your back and spine muscles. It also eases the tension in your shoulders, neck and back, which makes your body fully prepared for a flexibility workout.

You can perform it as illustrated in the previous chapter.

Flexibility Yoga Poses

Let us get started with:

1. Head To Knee Forward Bend (Janu Sirsasana)

Head to knee forward fold works wonders when it comes to improving your flexibility. This pose usually stretches your groin, hamstrings, shoulders and spine while strengthening your back muscles and massaging your abdominal organs. This hugely increases your flexibility. In fact, if you can touch your feet at first when you start, this pose will help you to do that in less than two weeks if you practice 2-3 times per week.

Here is how to do it:

1. Start in a seated position on the floor with your feet together and stretched forward.
2. Gently bend your left knee and bring your sole to your left foot thigh.
3. Slightly bend your upper body and stretch forward.

4. Extend your hands and grab your right foot (as a beginner this may be hard for you so you are allowed to use a yoga strap to grab your right foot)

5. Hold that position for 30 seconds to 1 minute. Switch legs and repeat the whole process. do 2 reps.

1. Standing Half Forward Bend (Ardha Uttanasana)

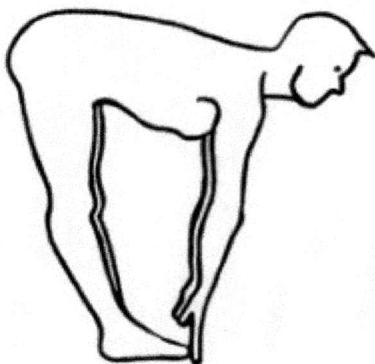

This pose normally focuses on stretching and strengthening your front torso and back as it improves your posture. Once you are done with head to forward knee bend you need to transition into this pose.

Here is how it is done:

1. Start in a standing position with your feet close together.
2. Keep your back straight and your butt up as you slowly lower your upper body.
3. Stop when you reach a point where your lower back starts to bend. As a beginner, that point can come before you even get to touch your knees but that should not worry you as you will improve, as you get more flexible.
4. Hold that pose for 30 seconds. Do 2 reps.

1. Lunge

This pose is a good hip opener that stretches your hips while working on different areas of your hips. It stretches your inner hip muscles, which makes you flexible enough even to do splits. Its effectiveness is what makes it ideal to be your third flexibility yoga exercise.

Perform it exactly the way you were taught in the previous chapter.

1. Pigeon Pose

Now that your inner hip muscles have been stretched, its time for you to stretch your outer hip muscles and nothing does that best than the pigeon pose. This pose is amazing for flexibility because it does not just stretch your thighs but also stretches your psoas, back and groin, which just go on to make you more flexible.

In case you have forgotten how to perform it, go to the previous chapters and see how.

1. Upward Facing Dog

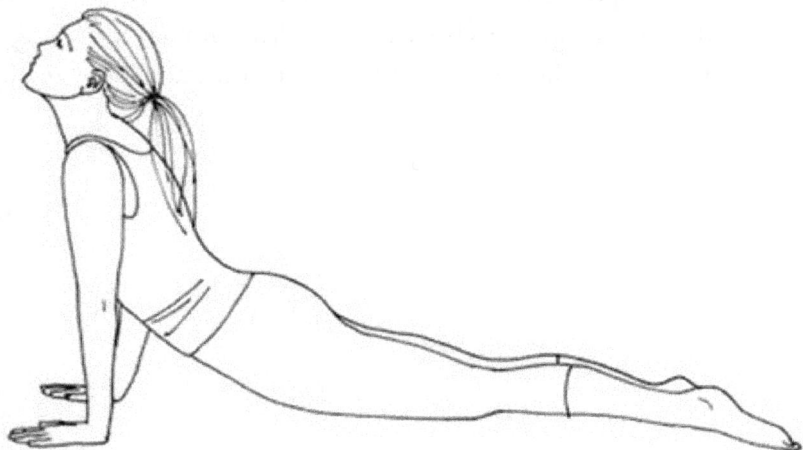

This pose increases your upper body flexibility by stretching your abdomen, shoulders and chest while strengthening your spine, arms and wrist. Its ability to open up your chest improves your posture when you are sitting on a desk probably in front of a computer or when doing seated and standing yoga pose.

The upward facing dog pose can be mistaken for a cobra pose because of their similarities. That said, they are not the same; one notable difference is how in upward facing dog pose you straighten your arms completely.

Here is how it is done;

1. Start by lying down on your stomach with your feet stretched back hip distance apart.
2. Place your palms beside your ribs in a position where your elbows form a 90-degree angle.
3. Press your palms firmly as you breathe in and slowly straighten

your arms to lift your upper body off the ground. Your shoulders should be directly over your wrists and your leg muscles should be engaged to keep your thighs off the floor.

4. Pick a spot to gaze at in front and maintain that gaze as you draw your shoulders back and your heart forward.

5. Hold on to the pose for 30 seconds to 1 minute. Do 4 reps.

1. Camel Pose (Ustrasana)

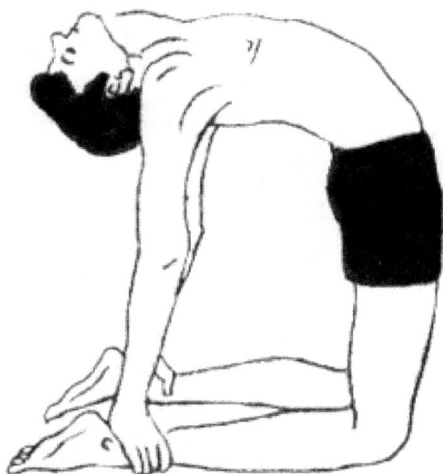

The camel pose is a good backbend pose to do after an upward facing dog because it stretches the entire front of your body and increases your level of flexibility. This pose enables you to get in a deep spinal extension without you necessarily having to support your upper body weight with your arms. The spinal extension brings mobility to your spine and increases its flexibility. As it does that, it also opens up your chest, stretches your abdominal wall and shoulders and strengthens your legs, glutes, back and neck.

Here is how to do it:

1. Start on your knees. Your legs should be hip width apart.
2. Slowly engage your core as you raise your hands and lower them towards your back as if you wanted to touch your butt. As you lower your hands, lift your chest to enable you to go as far as you possibly can. As a beginner, you might not be able to reach down and touch your heels so just go as far as you can

and hold. You will get there as you become flexible.

3. Let your head hang backward and gaze on the back for 30 seconds to 1 minute. Do 4 reps.

4. Go back to your starting position by slowly bringing your hands from the back to your glutes, exhale and lift your hips up.

Cool Down

Easy Pose

You should end your flexibility session with a relaxing yoga pose that will help you meditate and think about the benefits that the poses you have done have brought to your body. The perfect cool down pose is the easy pose. Easy pose is a classic meditative pose, which is good at slowing down your metabolism, straightening your spine and calming your mind; which is what you need when cooling down.

If you find it hard to hold on to an easy pose because you are used to having a chair that supports your back, you can make the pose more comfortable by placing a folded blanket under your butt.

You can start with those basic yoga routines. Now, yoga normally goes hand in hand with injuries. That said, there are methods that you can actually use to prevent injury and it is important to know them.

How To Prevent Yoga Injuries

It is important to do the following to prevent injuries:

1. *Warm-up*

One of the best ways that you can use to avoid injuries in yoga is by doing warm-ups before a yoga routine. Many people who get injuries from yoga get those injuries because they go straight into a full yoga routine. Why is this bad?

Almost every yoga routine comprises of yoga poses that make you do some deep stretches. If you are not prepared for them, the stretches can trigger your muscles protective reflexes and cause you to suffer from pulls and strains.

To avoid such injuries, you need to prepare your body for strenuous workouts and the only way to do that is by starting your yoga session with a set of warm-up poses. Warming up releases stress from your muscles and makes them flexible and ready for intense stretches. Therefore, make going to a yoga class 10-15 minutes early so that you can do some warm-up exercises your daily habit.

1. *Use Props*

Most people get yoga injuries because they don't usually get into the right postures when doing yoga. This is most common with beginners like you who are less flexible and unable to correctly do some yoga poses.

Props are great for avoiding injuries because they help you get into right positions. For example, if you perform a pose like bridge the wrong way, you will surely hurt your back. However if you use a prop by placing let's say a block under your butt when performing a bridge, the prop will help you perform the pose correctly and that will automatically help you avoid a back injury that you might have had.

1. *Have some private lessons*

As you may know by now, yoga poses are all about alignment and angles. One of the reasons why you may be injured while doing yoga is because you perform a yoga pose while on wrong alignment and angle. When that happens, your muscles are usually stressed and end up getting injured. A good example of that is the common scenario of people who perform a downward dog without their lower back being lengthened. Normally this is caused by having their legs and torso meeting in obtuse. This scenario usually results in a back injury.

One of the ways you can avoid such injuries is by arranging some private sessions with a good yoga teacher who can take you through different poses teaching you how to perform them the right way.

1. *Listen to your body*

This might come as a surprise to you but listening to your body actually helps you avoid injuries. Let me break it down for you. When you are in a yoga class, you usually take your cues from what you see the yoga teacher doing. For instance, when your yoga teacher folds his/her body to illustrate a pose you automatically follow his/her footsteps and do the same.

However, sometimes what you see from the outside is not always right for your body especially if you are a beginner. You can try to copy the teacher and do a headstand but if you are not ready for it, you will definitely end up with one or more injuries. Therefore, the best thing to do to avoid injuries is simply listening to your body. Yoga usually helps us to be more aware of our bodies and ourselves. Use that to find out if a pose is right for you or not.

1. Stop competing

Your level of success in yoga is not measured by how great you are at doing all the poses that your teacher does. It is also not measured by the rate at which you outdo your classmates rather it is measured by how you can personally grow.

When you lose sight of that and start trying to keep up with everyone around you the only thing that you will gain are injuries because you will push your body beyond its limit. Therefore, to avoid these types of injuries, you need to stop competing and just focus on your personal growth.

Now you are ready to start practicing yoga. But before you do, take a look at the chapter below to learn what you are supposed to eat when practicing yoga.

Buy the Audio version of this book by clicking here:
https://itunes.apple.com/us/audiobook/
yoga-for-beginners-your-guide-to-master-yoga-poses/
id1441152740

Section 5: Yoga Diet

A yoga teacher in California once said that eating is the single most important thing when you are practicing yoga, which is very true. Just like cars need fuel so does our body need food to function.

In yoga, what you eat matters a lot because a balanced and calm mind does not just happen because of practicing yoga, it does so because you have properly nourished your body with the right food. Without eating right, it is hard for you to see the benefits of yoga in your life. Which brings us to the question, how do you nourish yourself properly? What are you supposed to eat as a yogi?

One of the most influential yoga practitioners in India is called Patanjali. Pantanjali practiced yoga and he ate tons of kales cooked with olive oil and spirulina smoothies. Pantanjali had written a guidebook of classical yoga called yoga Sutra and what was surprising about this book is it did not mention any specific list of foods to eat when you are practicing yoga. The yoga book Bhagavad Gita didn't mention any type of foods to follow in yoga either. Does this mean there is no prescribed menu of what to eat like a yogi?

This might not be what you expected to hear from this chapter but it is true, there is no one recognized food list for yogis to follow.

While there is no food list to follow, a yoga diet actually exists. What is this yoga diet? This diet is all about how the foods you eat make you feel rather than foods that you need to eat. The yoga diet is any meal or ingredient that nourishes and clears your mind, keeps your body light and enhances some clarity and lightness in your body. In short, it is any diet that makes your body strong or ideal for practicing yoga; any diet that makes your system feel supported rather than depleted when you practice yoga.

So how can you come up with this yogic diet?

The Yogic diet is most often than not mistaken for a vegan diet but that is not what it is. So what does a yogic diet mean exactly and how do

141

you come up with one? To create a yogic diet, you only need to follow some few basic rules.

Here they are:

- It shouldn't have chemicals and stimulants

The first rule that you must adhere to when creating your own yogic diet is your foods or ingredients shouldn't contain any chemicals or stimulants. Why? The reason why this is so is that foods and drinks like artificial sweeteners, alcohol, tobacco and caffeine provide your body with chemicals which alters your mind and affects its level of concentration.

- It should be Sattvic

Sattvic is a Sanskrit word that means purity or light. 'Your yogic diet needs to be sattvic' basically means your diet needs to be life-giving to your body, mind and spirit. How?

In the Ayurvedic (medical science of ancient India) philosophy, there are normally 3 gunas (qualities) of everything in nature. One is Sattva (purity and harmony), Tama (bland, lethargic and slow) and Raja (fast, hot and spicy). These three qualities are what need to be in your diet for it to be sattvic. That said, the diet doesn't just need them to be present, it needs them to be balanced for them to make one quality diet. Here is an elaboration of each quality:

Rajasic food; these are foods that are hot, bitter, spicy, salty and dry. These types of foods normally stimulate your mind and excite your passions and they include herbs and spices.

Tamasic food; this quality includes bland foods like fermented foods, onions, garlic, tobacco and meat.

Sattvic food; this is the diet that is ideal for you as a yoga student. The sattvic food leads to true health, a fit body and a peaceful mind. It also has a balanced flow of energy between your body fitness and mind.

Some of the Sattvic foods include honey and herb teas, sprouted seeds, seeds, nuts, legumes, butter and cheese, milk, pure fruit juices, fresh fruit and vegetables and whole-meal bread.

- *You should practice ahimsa*

The word ahimsa means nonviolence. Practicing ahimsa means eating foods that do not harm other human beings, the environment and animals. Basically, your yogic food must be conscious of the environment and others.

- *Your meals should be properly timed*

The Yogic diet is not just about what you eat it is also about when you eat. Let me break it down for you. Your body normally utilizes its energy in anticipation to the time that you have trained it to eat. For example, if you eat 7 a.m and 12 pm your body will use more energy when you approach your eating hours because it is used to receiving more energy around that time.

So how should you time your food? The best thing to do is to avoid eating two hours before exercising and going to sleep. This normally helps your body to function better because you give your body time to digest food. If you were to exercise immediately after eating you would be using the energy for digestion to exercise. When it comes to sleeping, eating 2 hours before sleep enables you to sleep with a clear mind because the hormones you will produce at night will be used to repair your damaged tissues rather than being used for digestion.

- *It should be high in vegetables*

One of the reasons why few people become vegetarians is because we think the only way we will get an ideal source of protein is when we eat meat. However, is that the only way and is it the best way to get proteins?

You might not know this but meat has the worst protein quality. This is because the meat we eat normally contains uric acid. Why is that bad? Your liver is usually not able to completely break down and dispose of uric acid so what it does is it dumps the remaining uric acid to your tissues and joints. That is not just unhealthy but dangerous to your body, as it can cause diseases like cancer and arthritis.

Vegetarians get the best quality of proteins because vegetables don't have uric acid. Some of the high-quality protein vegetables include legumes, leafy greens, nuts and dairy products.

Yoga diet is about foods which support your body and not about foods which can destroy or are unhealthy to your body like meat; that's it is recommended to be vegetarian.

- *It should give you some break from food.*

For your body to be healthy and able to support you better when doing yoga exercises, you should give it an off day in eating and let it detoxify. To detoxify, you need to choose a day where you will do a full day fast. That will help you purify and reenergize your mind and body.

Those are the basic guidelines that can help you come up with your own yogic diet. But why should you make your own yogic diet? Isn't there just a standard yogic diet that we all can follow when we are doing yoga?

The answer is no. Let me explain. As you may know by now, yoga is a personal exercise. People do yoga for different reasons and that's why it is not a one size fits all kind of exercise. Here everyone has a particular thing that works best for them. Yoga diet is no different. It is personal too. Why? This is because what you may need is not what another person needs. In fact what you may need right now is not what you will need 3 years from now. Needs change and that's why it's hard to come up with one yogic diet that is written on stone. Therefore, you have to find yourself a diet that works for you by listening to your body and finding out not just what you like but what you need for you to be healthy and strong for yoga. That said your yoga diet must always be set according to the values and philosophical teachings of yoga.

So where should you start when looking for your own yogic diet?

The best way to create your own yogic diet is in practicing mindful eating. By mindful eating, I mean having an open-minded awareness of what you choose to eat and how it affects you.

Thus, what you should do is to start trying those eating systems that are appealing to you one at a time and then see if they are good for you. But, how do you know a certain type of eating system is good for you? As you continue practicing yoga and eating, you will start getting a natural sense of what is good for your body and what is bad. For instance, if you eat a certain type of food and then your energy starts going down, your sleep gets shorter and you start experiencing stomach problems that you didn't have before, you will automatically know that a particular system of eating is not good for you.

On the other hand, if your sleep improves, your energy levels increase and you feel great during and long after you have eaten a certain type of food, you will know that is the perfect food system for you and then stick with it.

Thus, what to eat when doing yoga all depends on you, your body needs and how your body reacts to the food you eat. To find the perfect food you should explore different types of foods and then listen to your body and let it teach you the best yogic diet for you.

What Should You Eat Before And After A Yoga Workout?

As you now know, yoga exercises are as important as the meals that you eat when you are practicing yoga and for you to get the best out of your yoga exercise you need to know how to balance the two. The most crucial part that you need to balance the two is before and after yoga. This is because getting this process wrong at that time can affect the outcome of your exercise. Therefore, you need to learn what is best for you to eat before and after yoga practice.

What To Eat Before Yoga Workout

Watermelon

There are two possible things, which can affect your yoga workouts. One is hunger and the second one is dehydration that comes from sweating and losing excess water in the body. Watermelon is one of the best foods to eat before a workout because it helps you curb both hunger and dehydration. Watermelon is made up of water, which increases water levels in your body keeping you hydrated. The water also keeps you feeling full for longer.

Almonds

Yoga just like any other exercise needs a lot of energy for you to perform it effectively. One of the foods that you can take to boost your energy is almonds. Almonds contain magnesium, potassium and vitamin E, which are all nutrients that help in boosting your energy. So grab a handful of almonds preferably unsalted the next time you feel like you need more energy to workout.

Bananas

The other food that is good to have before yoga is a banana. Bananas are usually rich in potassium. When you eat a banana, its potassium works with sodium in your body to help you stay hydrated which is very important when you are working out.

Whole-grain toast

When you practice yoga in a completely empty stomach, most often than not you will get tummy rumbles that are not just irritating but distractive to. You can avoid those tummy rumbles by taking a whole grain toast 2 hours before your workout. What the toast does is it provides you with energy that can sustain you throughout your whole workout and a stomach that is not empty hence no rumbles.

Oatmeal

Oatmeal is a good pre-workout snack to take. This is because it is light and easy for your body to burn but strong enough to provide you with enough energy to carry you through your entire workout.

Apple

Apples are good to take before a yoga class because they contain water which can help in hydrating your body. They also contain fiber, which can help you not to feel hungry faster.

Greek yogurt

Greek yogurt is a protein-rich food that is good at keeping you energetic the whole time you are doing yoga. Greek yogurt does that because it contains lactose, a type of sugar that your body uses to provide you with energy.

What To Eat After A Yoga Workout

When you finish your workout, you obviously aren't allowed to eat anything in the next 30 minutes. That was explained earlier on in the audiobook. Nevertheless, the good news is that you are free to eat after the thirty minutes. But, what should you eat?

Yoga practices have been known to cause dehydration so the first thing that you will need to take is water. If you are not a fun of water, then you can squeeze some lemon or blend some mango, avocado, passions or pineapples to create a juice that will keep you hydrated.

Yoga doesn't just dehydrate you, it also uses up all your stored glycogen, which leaves your body with a decrease in energy levels. This situation is dangerous because it can cause your metabolism to slow as well as cause muscle loss if you don't eat and provide your body with energy. Here is a list of some of the best foods that can provide your body with energy after a yoga workout:

- Fruit salad
- Artichoke
- Quinoa
- Brown rice
- Broccoli
- Raspberries
- Blueberries
- Sweet potatoes
- Cereals
- Whole grain or brown rice
- Dark leafy greens
- Beets
- Chocolate milk
- Sandwich

You now know how to eat when you are practicing yoga. The next chapter will focus on frequently asked questions and their answers. This topic is important because it gives you a heads up on the world of yoga as you get to see some of the possible questions that you might have, being answered.

Buy the Audio version of this book by clicking here: https://itunes.apple.com/us/audiobook/ [yoga-for-beginners-your-guide-to-master-yoga-poses/](https://itunes.apple.com/us/audiobook/yoga-for-beginners-your-guide-to-master-yoga-poses/) [id1441152740](https://itunes.apple.com/us/audiobook/yoga-for-beginners-your-guide-to-master-yoga-poses/id1441152740)

Section 6: Frequently Asked Questions

As a beginner, it is only natural for you to have a 'million and one' questions about yoga. We all do when we start a new thing.

This chapter is going to try to answer possible questions that you might have by highlighting some of the frequently asked questions about yoga. This list will cover some of the questions that you might have and any other questions that you never thought of asking. You will then get answers that will not only satisfy your curiosity but also make you a better yogi. Without further ado, let's look at these questions and answers;

Q: What is the age limit for practicing yoga?

A: Many people stay away from yoga because they think they are either too young or too old for yoga. The truth of the matter is anyone and everyone can practice yoga as long as they are old enough to stand and communicate. Mostly the age limit for yoga starts from 5 years up until the age where you can't move your body because of old age and this is usually from 80 years onwards. Otherwise, it doesn't matter if you are weak, strong, skinny or overweight, you can practice yoga perfectly.

Furthermore, yoga classes are categorized into different group of classes which make people of different ages feel more comfortable. For instance, there are yoga classes for women only, men only, children only and old people.

Q: Should you still do yoga when you are on your periods?

A: This question always causes a huge debate whenever it is brought up. There has never been a clear answer to this question. This is because there are several different schools of thoughts when it comes to yoga and periods. Some experts believe that woman who are having their menses, should rest because their bodies need to cleanse and detoxify themselves and the last thing they need when doing that is stress that comes from a workout. Other experts believe it is okay for women to do yoga when having their menses because yoga postures do not cause lasting harm.

I think the middle ground between the two schools of thoughts works perfectly. Yes, there are no yoga poses that can cause you lasting harm but there are other poses that can either hurt you or interfere with your natural blood flow when you practice them when on your menses. So what you should do is to simply listen to your body, if you feel your body is strong enough for yoga then go right ahead and do it but go easy and avoid yoga poses that may cause you harm like a full wheel, seated spinal twist, a breath of fire, handstand and shoulder stand pose. If your body doesn't feel like doing yoga, then respect this and rest.

Q: How many times should I practice yoga to see some benefit?

A: The best thing that you can ever do in order to see some benefit from yoga is to get started in yoga. I know you may have expected me to tell you how many times per week you need to practice to see some results but yoga doesn't work that way. It is a journey that you need to take one step at a time for you to grow into a level where your body can enjoy the benefits of yoga.

That said, as a beginner in yoga, you will notice some benefits of yoga when you start regardless of whether you are doing it once, twice or thrice a week. As a newbie, you should first focus on getting used to yoga poses. After that, you should slowly start adding the number of times that you do yoga in a week. Once you get to that level, your body will then start to enjoy the numerous benefits of yoga.

So your goal should be to ease into an advanced point of yoga where you will enjoy constant benefit rather than think how many times you need to do yoga per week to benefit from it.

Q: Can yoga help me lose weight?

A: The answer is yes but not in the way that you think.

Yoga is a whole body workout, which makes you work hard, sweat and feel exhausted. That alone can help you lose some weight. But yoga also uses challenging physical exercises to tone your body and improve your health through heightened flexibility, relaxation and body awareness which is another way that you can lose weight. Apart from those two, yoga also makes you get in touch with your body which helps you make healthier decisions about what you eat; a situation that also helps you to lose weight.

That said, yoga is not a good cardio workout; it is not an activity that burns a lot of calories. Hence, when you start practicing yoga, you will lose some weight but not too much.

Q: What is the difference between yoga and other conventional exercises?

A: Conventional exercise is any physical activity that cultivates, arouses and strengthens the vital organs of your body, but yoga is simply a discipline that mainly focuses on integrating your physical, mental and spiritual fitness. In short, yoga is more than a physical body workout as it emphasizes on matching your breath with your movement, which provides you with spiritual and mental benefits.

Q: Can overweight people practice yoga?

A: Today's society has painted a picture that depicts yoga as an activity that only involves slender and extremely fit people. This has created a misconception that overweight people cannot do yoga, which is not true because overweight people can do yoga perfectly. All you have to do if you are overweight is to look for a small class when looking for a yoga class. Why? You will need more assistance when doing yoga postures and the best way you can get that assistance is when attending a small class where the teacher can easily assist you as he/she has fewer people to focus on.

If you are overweight, you also need to be patient with yourself. Yes, yoga improves your flexibility but that doesn't happen instantly. Thus, if you are unable to perform a pose don't be disappointed, just opt out, do what you can and with no time you will be able to do what you thought was impossible.

Q: Will yoga interfere with my religious beliefs?

A: Quite a number of people think that chanting Sanskrit slogans in a yoga class means you are shifting your faith to another religion; first of all, switching religions is not that easy and secondly, that's totally false. There is no way yoga interferes with your religion. Many people have been practicing yoga for years and no one has ever come out and said a yoga teacher persuaded them to change their religious beliefs and I bet you will never come across such a case.

Yoga means union. What you do during yoga is uniting your soul, body and mind. This does not lead you to a different religious path it only enhances your spiritual beliefs. Therefore, if you are a Christian it enhances your Christianity the same happens to Muslims, Hindus and others. However, if you feel uncomfortable with the yoga chants it's best for you to find a class that doesn't have Sanskrit chants.

Q: Will I get stares in class because I am new to yoga?

A: Yoga classes are not harsh to newbies as many people think. In fact they are the opposite. A yoga class is normally very friendly. Yogis treat each other like family and so as a newbie, you get multiple helping hands rather than stares.

Buy the Audio version of this book by clicking here:
    https://itunes.apple.com/us/audiobook/
yoga-for-beginners-your-guide-to-master-yoga-poses/
id1441152740

Conclusion

We have come to the end of the book. Thank you for listening and congratulations on listening until the end.

I can't emphasize this enough; yoga is one of the best exercises around. It is soothing, relaxing and very beneficial to you. All you have to do is just try it and have an open mind and you will wonder why no one told you about it before.

Thank you,
Emily Oddo

Buy the Audio version of this book by clicking here:
https://itunes.apple.com/us/audiobook/
yoga-for-beginners-your-guide-to-master-yoga-poses/
id1441152740

Sneak Preview of Mindfulness Buddhism

I would like to share with you a free sneak peek to another one of my audiobooks that I think you will really enjoy. The audiobook is called "Mindfulness Buddhism- Your Practical and Easy Guide to Be Peaceful, Relieve Stress, Anxiety and Depression Right Now!" and it's about how mindfulness can make a difference in your life, dealing with stress, anxiety and depression. Enjoy!

Chapter 1: Meditation Basics

What Meditation Actually Is and What it Isn't

When picturing how meditation is done, most people would imagine having to sit in lotus position while keeping his eyes closed and breathing "Ohm!" in a sort of trance. And when asked what goes on inside, it is a common conception that the mind is free or is being freed of any thought or emotion.

Such an image isn't particularly wrong, but it isn't the only method of meditation, either. There are more than one type of meditation technique, and one lets the person focus on a specific object. Instead of keeping the mind blankly fixated on this thing or idea, the mind familiarizes itself with it. And in this audiobook, this type of meditation shall be further discussed in the succeeding pages.

It may now thus occur to you that people actually meditate every day. When, for example, a person focuses on a certain object or matter, scrutinizes its advantages and disadvantages, and then enumerates the benefits he will reap from it, he practices meditation.

Illustration:

Buying a car requires weeks, or perhaps months, of contemplation. The process would commonly start with the establishment of the needs the buyer, and then followed by the determination of which car type will best serve this need. Afterwards, the buyer will research on the differences or advantages offered by each car brand. He could read reviews on the internet, prod friends with the same car type to reveal problems, or talk to car dealers about the best value for their money.

After gathering sufficient information, the buyer will now weigh the options in his mind. As he develops an inclination towards one, his desire to possess this specific brand and type of car deepens.

And as illustrated above, the essential exercise of contemplating which car to buy already results to meditation. Analytical processes may vary from person to person, but the same is true when selecting a university to enter, a house or apartment to live in, or more commonly, when selecting a person to marry. In fact, the very act of purchasing this audiobook constitutes a part of meditation.

Because meditation can be exercised on any object, may it be concrete or abstract, it can also be done anywhere. It may be done while in the car, during a commute, while engaging in crafts, or while sitting alone on the sofa at home.

It is not necessary to find a darkened room or an airy garden to have to practice meditation. This audiobook is all about practicality, hence the methods for meditation it shall discuss are those which will require no extra formal effort from the reader. It will instead focus on the substantial aspect of the practice.

Meditation as a Tool for the Perpetuation of Unvirtuous Thoughts

After having learned of the simplicity of meditation, a question now succeeds: "If I meditate every day, why am I still experiencing stress, anxiety or depression?"

This is because most people focus their mental efforts towards unvirtuous acts rather than virtuous ones.

Illustration:

When stuck in traffic, instead of focusing on the virtue of patience, the person is more likely to contemplate on the stupidity of the system, the incompetence of the traffic enforcers, the inconvenience from the construction happening on the street ahead, or the drivers who have caused the jam.

Many are not aware of its effect, but feeding this negative thought only strengthens the resolve and results only to greater stress. The simple idea that "the traffic enforcers are stupid" may evolve to, "they aren't doing their job properly", then to "my taxes are going to waste with these blokes". Feeding the thought further shall transform to anger. And should traffic persists, a circumstance outside the control of anyone stuck in it, anger can only ball up to stress and weigh down the spirits of the person.

Another example which every person may relate to better is thinking how much contempt they have over another. And in most cases, the subject of this contempt is one's boss.

This little seed of negativity will burrow deep in the crevices of the mind and shall be nurtured by every little observable fault the person does.

The emotion will find its way to the heart when it is shared with others. Hatred will bloom once, during his meditations, the person integrates his or her thoughts with what he or she learned from others.

These strong negative emotions are like poison inflicted upon one's self. It destroys no one but the person who harbors them. No one has died from anger or hatred, but these and others of the same kind invite stress, and later on, despair and depression. And when discussing these emotions with other people, instead of relieving oneself of the weight, he does the opposite.

It is easier to meditate upon all the bad things in life the same way it is easier to love junk food than vegetables. There are no explanations yet as to why, or if there is, it's not in this audiobook, but you will discover later on that to cultivate peace through meditation, the mind undergoes the same process.

More than Listening

Before discussing the actual practice of meditation, understand that by choosing and listening this audiobook, you have already started.

Meditation is a mental exercise, but unlike those geared towards improving aptitude, knowing is not enough. Upon reading the texts of this audiobook, you would have gained intelligence. Peace, and thus relief from stress, anxiety and depression, however, is developed through discipline.

To help you practice this mental discipline as early as now, exercises and their corresponding guidelines will be supplied throughout the audiobook. You may choose to do them or not. But should you opt for the latter, this audiobook implores that you subject its words under critical analysis. Do not take them as they are, and instead, ask yourself a thousand different why's.

Why are Buddhist principles discussed when I only need to know how to meditate?

Why is this audiobook *so abstract when I was expecting it to be more concrete; like help me give an alternative to the lotus position?*

Why are the roots of my depression being discussed when I only want relief?

Why does this audiobook *say I shouldn't settle in unvirtuous thoughts, but it at the same time encourages me to think about them?*

Why is this audiobook *so long?*

Why does it seem that concepts are being discussed repetitively?

Why should I even believe what this audiobook *is saying?*

Why shouldn't I question the validity of everything it says?

Exercise 1:

What to do: Before moving to the next subchapter, take the time to think about the unvirtuous thoughts that you have entertained in the past. Below are some guide questions to help you identify what these are:

- Is there a person you hate, or is currently irritating you?

- Are there aspects of your job which you despise?

- Is there something about your special other that makes you want to break up with him or her?

- Are there things or matters within your family that encourage establishing and maintaining distance?

- Are there things about yourself you do not like?

- Is there anything in your daily life which you especially dislike, like the commute, the traffic, or the climate?

Important Note! If your answer to any of the above questions is in the affirmative, stop yourself from thinking any further. Like an open door that leads to a trap, the emotions associated with the objects asked about will pull you like gravity. And before you even know it, you will once again be snagged by and be drowning in unvirtuous thoughts.

Instead, however, stop before the door, refrain from crossing it, and calmly look at the view inside. *"Yes, there is a person I hate at the moment,"* and **stop!** Do not let the hateful thought—the very substance of this emotion—follow. But should it be inevitable, let it pass by as if you are watching a passing cloud, and then move on to the next door.

Objective: This exercise is like a precursor to meditation. It seeks to develop objectivity in the mind. Although it doesn't help you diminish emotions completely, which is absolutely impossible, it allows your mind to stay analytical without being influenced by feelings.

Buy the Audio version of this book by clicking here:

https://itunes.apple.com/us/audiobook/
mindfulness-buddhism-your-practical-easy-guide-to-be/id1440641421

Chapter 2: Analytical Meditation

Focusing on a Single Object

Much like how the brain works when contemplating on the purchase of a car, the mind becomes critical in analytical meditation. And unlike in daily mental musings where the mind jumps from one thought to another, this method of meditation requires that all critical analysis be focused on one object only.

The object can be something that the senses can affect, like breathing. And it can also be an abstract concept such as patience.

Process: Begin the meditation by critically familiarizing yourself with the object. If, for example, the object is patience, you may start your analysis by contemplating on its benefits.

- How will patience affect a certain circumstance? Will it change according to your will? Or will it stay the same?

- If you remain patient on a given situation, like traffic, what thoughts would be running through your head instead?

- Does patience come with scientifically proven health benefits?

These questions do not need immediate answering if the answers haven't revealed themselves yet. Questioning, in fact, already constitutes critical analysis. What's important in this initial step is that you start the ball rolling.

Afterwards, try to expand your analysis beyond the benefits.

- Can patience be practiced only by silence? Or is there a way of practicing it whereby you express what's on your mind?

- Harboring patience can change or control a person's mood. But is there a way of using patience to influence the behavior of people around?

Important Note! Keep in mind of the requisite of staying focused on the single object. By asking questions and trying to answer them, different ideas and thoughts will rise. And eventually, you may find yourself in the middle of chasing another object.

Thinking is easy. It's what the brain does from the moment you wake to the second you fall asleep. The difficult part in meditation is trying to stay focused on this single object. This is where discipline will be practiced.

Of course, in your meditations, the questions you've come up with must be answered. Researching for answers from audiobooks or online resources is alright. Answering the questions subjectively is fine as well. But as what this audiobook has encouraged you to do, go beyond knowing. Be critical with everything you read or know.

Illustration:

In the first question, if the circumstance is being stuck in traffic, the obvious answer is that patience will change nothing. It will not clear the road for you; that is a fact. But go beyond this knowledge by thinking, "Hey! Neither does anger. Traffic is something I cannot control, after all." And then compare and weigh patience against anger. Think of how they would affect your mood, and how it will then affect your day, and how it will affect your behavior towards other people.

If, on the other hand, the circumstance is having to deal with a barista in Starbucks not working at your ideal pace, patience again will not change anything. And then it might occur to you that expressing exasperation will. Alerted by your loud indignant voice, and alarmed by the sight of your knitted eyebrows, the slow barista might just get the kick he needs to double time. You must expand, however, your musings to what's around you and the barista. Imagine how the people in Starbucks would react to the outburst. A group of girls might snicker in the corner while throwing meaningful glances at your direction. Other baristas might roll their eyes at the incident and make a mental note to avoid you in the future. And then imagine how you would feel if you catch any of these tiny and silent reactions.

And then think of how the scene might've changed if you instilled patience instead. The people in Starbucks would have continued with whatever they were doing and not realize your existence. The baristas would not have cared who you are. But you did, however, maintained the peace within you.

Goal: The goal in analytical meditation is to empathize or develop a certain closeness with the object, and then apply this new sense of familiarity of the object whenever apt.

Like researching on the benefits, specs and reviews of a certain car, the more you know, the more you feel captivated by it. At some point even, you will feel personally attached to it. And when, for example, you are faced by an adverse opinion of it, because you know every single detail of the car, you may rebut the claim with a well-constructed and logical counter-statements. You might also react to the adversity by agreeing to it because you recognize and accept its flaws.

Illustration:

Following the example in the previous topic, which is patience, the goal is to not simply know the answers to the questions you have initially set forth. You must also aim to combine positive emotions with the object, and then apply them whenever necessary.

Going back to the Starbucks example, say you are stuck between staying patient and bursting into anger. If you choose to stay patient—to not say a word—but cannot control the raging fire inside, then your meditation has not helped you reach your objective. Your inner peace was still disturbed because you only know that patience is a virtue, and that it is the right choice. However, this virtue has not yet been instilled as yours, which is why the negative emotion remained.

If, however, during your meditations you were able to fully empathize with patience; that you were able to develop a closeness to it that it seems you are the embodiment of patience itself, then you wouldn't even reach that point where you have to choose between staying patient and bursting into anger.

Objective: What good will come out of this method of overthinking? You get to discover the truth on your own. And when the truth has bloomed from your heart and mind on its own, no one will be able to take it away from you, hence the critical analysis.

Illustration:

It is similar with introducing religion to a person. A child will believe God exists if told. However, upon reaching adulthood, this belief would also have been easy to take away given enough knowledge to believe otherwise.

A critical person, before completely throwing his beliefs through the window, would first question. *Is God real?* Similar with what has been discussed in this audiobook, the person will undergo meditation. He will seek the truth through critical analysis.

This is a personal journey. Although mentors and audiobook such as this one may guide the person, everything will still be subjected under his scrutiny. Once however the journey is complete, the truth will naturally bloom from the heart.

Later on, whenever faced with adverse evidence or knowledge, his belief and his peace will not be disturbed because he knows in his heart what is true.

Important Note! Because in analytical meditation the person remains critical in his familiarization with the object, he has the option to choose one of the subjects incited in Exercise 1.

Instead, however, of looking outward and at the person, practice inward reflection. Drop the habit of finding more reasons to feel contempt. Instead, try to understand why you feel that way. Ask yourself why you think his actions annoy you when others, despite having the same faults, do not.

If your contempt is great, and the emotions associated with it rise, take control of it by applying what you have learned in Exercise 1. And then continue with your meditation.

Where and When to Practice: As previously discussed, meditation can be done anywhere and at any time. It can even be done concurrently with other activities. However, for the purposes of this audiobook, you are encouraged to dedicate a specific time of the day for the practice.

If you live on your own, the perfect times would be in the morning immediately after waking up, and in the evening right before sleeping. And you may meditate on your bed if you can manage to stay awake for 15 minutes. If not, then choose any part of your home where you can focus and hear nothing but your thoughts.

If, on the other hand, you live with others, or if there are kids in the house, find a 15-minute period on your daily schedule where you are sure you will not be bothered. Then if a quiet and private room would be impossible to find, try looking for peaceful spots in a nearby park. If that's impossible as well, go for an uncrowded coffee shop.

When meditating in a public place, drown the buzz of the crowd by listening to instrumental music. You run the risk of being mistaken for a felon if you sit in a corner intently staring at blank space, so bring a cup of drink with you to look less suspicious.

Important Notes!

• **15-minute period**: Initially, meditating for 5 to 6 minutes a day would be sufficient. The reason why you need to dedicate a longer time, however, is because getting into the meditative state requires more time.

The meditative state is achieved when you are able to push the noises in your head aside. And when you are ready to bring your selected object to the centerstage of your consciousness.

It may sound easy, but in reality, you will grapple with the urge to check your phone for new emails, or with the thought that this little time would be better dedicated to dealing with deadlines. And this is why the morning (immediately after waking up) is the most ideal time for meditation. Before the wave of errands comes crashing on your consciousness, you have already and successfully meditated.

• **Peace and quiet:** Even in the middle of the most crowded train or in the noisiest streets, people sometimes slip into a meditative state effortlessly. For this practice, however, the ideal environment is somewhere peaceful and quiet. This is because meditation requires immense discipline from you.

When you focus on an object, your brain gets too tired or bored that it starts chasing other thoughts. And unfortunately, a stimulus-rich environment offers the best distractions. One moment you could be at the brink of uncovering the root of patience, but then you saw a baby on a stroller and you suddenly remembered you have to buy diapers so you have to not forget to stop by at Costco after work, and taking advantage of the visit, you might as well buy eggs, bread, and coffee for breakfast tomorrow, which then reminds you of the laundry which needs pressing because you and the kids would have nothing to wear tomorrow.

Most importantly, because discipline is often associated with punishment, treat meditation as a form of relaxation. Look at it as that time of the day where you get to drop all worries on the ground; that very special 5 minutes you spend exclusively for your personal growth and well-being.

Exercise 2:

What to do: You will now fully engage in meditation. Opting for an object of your own choosing is ideal because no one knows best what beautiful truth should bloom in your heart. If you find the object challenging to meditate on, however, a less complex subject might be more beneficial. Below are some subjectively easy objects, and their corresponding guide questions to help you jumpstart the practice:

- *Romantic Love*

  ○ How do you know when you're in love? How do you distinguish the feeling from mere infatuation or lust?

  ○ Can man live without romantic love? And can his life be well lived even in its absence?

  ○ What is the root of romantic love? Is it inside the person who loves? Or is it the person he or she loves? Will love then be extinguished by the passing of the person being loved?

  ○ Can there only be one romantic love in a lifetime? Or is it possible to truly love more than one person? Is an "ultimate" love real?

- *Sorrow*

  ○ Why is it difficult to convert this emotion to acceptance? Is it even possible to convert it to acceptance?

  ○ Can sorrow be alleviated by something other than time?

  ○ How do you get by this powerful emotion? Do you drown yourself in alcohol? Do you lock yourself up in a darkened room? Do you talk to people about it?

○ If a person's happiness over something be greater, does that mean that the loss of this something stirs greater sorrow in return?

● *Death*

○ What is your relationship with death? Is it a friend, a foe, or a mere stranger?

○ Is it possible to feel grief and joy concurrently in the passing of a loved one?

○ What will life be without death? Would life even be worth living without it?

○ Is there a correlation between death and overpopulation? If there is, does this mean the world is out of balance?

● *War*

○ What is the purpose of war? Why do some men despise it, while others yearn for it?

○ Can there be war without death and damage?

○ Will humans even realize peace without having to go through war?

○ In the past, wars were started primarily to conquer territories. How have wars evolved from then? What do people fight for in modern wars?

Duration: Stick to this exercise for a week or two. For your first try, limit your meditation to 3 minutes. See how many times you've caught yourself drifting to unfocused thoughts. When you feel that you've already improved, increase the time by one minute.

Important Note! Prepare an alarm so you wouldn't have to anxiously glance at the clock during meditation. Make sure, however, to set the volume low and to select a less distressing tone. The mind needs to ease slowly out of meditation.

Remember, in preparing to enter the meditative state, you unload your worries one by one. It makes sense, therefore, that in leaving such a peaceful state, you load back your worries in the same manner. If your alarm creates distress in your mind, it will feel like the fire alarm broke out while you were enjoying a nice hot shower, and without thinking, you load the fridge on your back and run through the door while still naked.

Objective: Like how a novice pianist familiarizes himself with the keys, the objective of this exercise is to help you get to know your mind a little better. You will learn that your concentration has limits and that your mind is a difficult stallion to tame.

Buy the Audio version of this book by clicking here:
https://itunes.apple.com/us/audiobook/
mindfulness-buddhism-your-practical-easy-guide-to-be/id1440641421

Chapter 3: Zazen

Introduction to Formal Meditation

The meditation technique discussed in the previous chapter is purely substantive. It focuses on how the mind should regulate thoughts, and how it should focus on an object. As to how the body should be positioned during meditation—whether sitting down, standing up, leaning against a wall, or reclining on the bed, none was provided. The only inkling of form in analytical meditation is the time that is encouraged to be dedicated in a day. But even that isn't absolute; they are mere recommendation which you can opt to disregard.

Formal meditation, on the other hand, requires religious dedication and a sacred space to be practiced—pretty much like how most prayers are done. It often comes hand-in-hand with a set of principles and virtues the person is enjoined to embody, such as the case with Buddhism. And depending on the type of formal meditation, it often seeks to discipline both the mind and the body.

Between formal and informal meditation, the latter is more practical because it's easier to fit in any schedule. This makes it ideal for those with barely any time left for himself in a day. And because informal meditation is not too selective of location, it can be done in the most convenient of places, even in the bathroom.

If, however, you wish to improve your posture and your breathing, which also contributes in relieving stress, anxiety and depression, then opt for formal meditation.

Also, if in case you find informal meditation difficult to practice because of lack of structure, the opposite might be more suitable for you. The formal meditation which shall be discussed in this audiobook is, in fact, a lot simpler to perform because no critical analysis is required. It is less taxing and more relaxing.

Zazen

There is more than one type of formal meditation and each is associated with a specific discipline such as mindfulness and openness. Others go as far as focusing on the energies of the body and directing them to the heart, the core or wherever. But because this audiobook serves as a practical guide to meditation, it shall focus on the most practical of them all: Zazen.

Zazen is the method of meditation practiced by Zen Buddhists. Among the several types of meditation, this form greatly appeals to beginners because the concept is easy to understand, and the form is versatile enough to allow individuals with physical problems and difficulties to practice zen meditation. Also, because Zazen doesn't require practitioners to study a set of principles rooted in Buddhism, it can be practiced in conjunction with any type of religion.

Mental Discipline in Zazen

Interestingly, the difference between analytical meditation and Zazen isn't too wide. You also have to familiarize yourself with an object in the latter. Unlike in analytical meditation, however, where you can choose different objects in every session, the only object in Zazen is your breathing.

During Zen meditation, the practitioner sits and counts his breath. It's as easy as that; no critical analysis is needed. Of course, however, every discipline comes with a challenge, and in Zazen, it's living in the present.

According to Zen Buddhism, most people are trapped in either the past or the future. Those who settle in the past often feel depressed, thinking of what they could and should have changed to set the present right. Those who live in the future, on the other hand, are often visited by anxiety because they constantly think of what might and should be. In this very demanding world where expectations are constantly set and setting expectations has become a way of life; where people are trapped in a cycle of never ending tasks, moving onward to the next after finishing one, people actually forget to live in the present. They forget to take a break, and just appreciate the moment.

The idea behind Zazen, therefore, is to discipline the mind to set worries aside and simply be in the present.

Of course, because you'll be sitting the entire time in a quiet room, nothing exciting would be going on while "living the present." The discipline you apply during meditation, however, will eventually and naturally become a state of mind. You will learn to live the present even outside of meditation.

Perhaps, on your next trip to the tropics, instead of planning on what Instagram-worthy pics to take because you need a hundred likes and a dozen more followers, you will actually enjoy the sun, sand and sea. Instead of worrying that people will think you're cheap and ugly because you didn't post photos of you on a fancy boat looking pretty and sexy, feel the wind and the spray of the ocean on your face as you ride that boat.

Process: After assuming the proper posture, which shall be discussed in detail later, the practitioner regulates his breathing. There is no need to stick to a count even when there is a recommended rhythm. Simply inhale deep and exhale as you naturally do, keeping a regular rhythm. Being too technical with breathing will only take your concentration away from the substantial aspect of the practice.

Afterwards, pour your focus on counting your breath. Once you reach ten counts, repeat back to one.

A common misconception in Zen meditation is that you empty your mind. That, of course, is impossible because as long as the mind is awake, thoughts will come and go. In actuality, Zen meditation redirects your thoughts to your breathing. Once you are able to achieve this strenuous task, instead of reliving that horrible breakup in your head, you would hear the beat of your heart, the sound of air passing through your nostrils, and even the rush of blood through your veins. This is what it means to live in the moment.

All this may sound easy, but it actually isn't because as described earlier, the mind is a difficult stallion to tame. When left alone with no one but yourself, with nothing but the wall, and doing nothing but sit, the thoughts in your head starts talking louder and clearer. And the issue here is that you wouldn't even know you have been listening to them the entire practice. You will only notice that your consciousness has been drifting when you've already lost count of your breath, or when emotions start stirring in your heart.

Thought, of course, cannot be pushed aside or blocked. And when you try to fight your thoughts, the stronger they become. So what you should do when they rise is to let them pass. Watch them as if you're passing by the window of an appliance store, glancing at the videos being played on the TV displays. When it's over, calmly resume your count, and feel the rise and fall of your chest.

One danger brought by passing thoughts, however, is getting triggered by the emotion they are associated with. The sole image of an empty bed could, for example, remind you of a failed relationship. And this could unleash a waterfall of emotions including reactions to the entire experience which is either regret or loathing. Unfortunately, some people unconsciously grip and cling to these emotions.

There are two ways to deal with these emotions during Zen meditation.

First, similar with analytical meditation, you empathize. Upon the rise of these negative feelings, follow it up immediately with positive ones. Embrace them and realize that they are part of you now. You cannot, after all, extinguish the feeling the same way you cannot erase the memory.

After accepting the emotion, let them go as you exhale, then resume your count. Or if you've already lost count, start back at one.

Second, you watch these thoughts without judgement. Most Zen practitioners are able to maintain tranquility regardless of the thought that passes. And their secret in reaching this level of calmness is detachment.

Which of the two methods is more difficult is up to you to determine. Each person, after all, undergoes a unique meditation experience, and not everyone reacts the same to the rise of unwanted thoughts.

Buy the Audio version of this book by clicking here:
https://itunes.apple.com/us/audiobook/
mindfulness-buddhism-your-practical-easy-guide-to-be/id1440641421

CPSIA information can be obtained
at www.ICGtesting.com
Printed in the USA
LVHW012102090721
692310LV00018B/815

9 781393 652045